PROGRAM READY II

MORE
QUICK AND COMPLETE PROGRAMS FOR THE CHURCH YEAR

DOROTHY MacNEILL

THE UNITED CHURCH PUBLISHING HOUSE

Program Ready II
More Quick and Complete Programs for the Church Year

All biblical quotations, unless otherwise noted, are from the *New Revised Standard Version Bible*, copyright © 1989, by the Division of Christian Education of the National Council of the Churches of Christ in the United States of America.

The story of Tom and Anne Gunn, which appears in "22: A Golden Program" was taken from the book "A Rose In November" by Francene Gillis. Published by Daily Bread Publishing, Port Hood, Inv. Co., N.S. B0E 2W0. Used by Permission.

Every reasonable effort has been made to find copyright holders. The publisher would be pleased to have any errors or omissions brought to its attention.

Canadian Cataloguing in Publication Data

MacNeill, Dorothy, 1934-

    Program ready II

Includes bibliographical references.
ISBN 1-55134-061-5

1. Worship programs. 2. Church year. I. Title.

BV198.M323 1996   264   C96-931602-X

The United Church Publishing House
3250 Bloor St. West, 4th floor
Etobicoke, Ontario, Canada
M8X 2Y4
(416) 231-5931

Printed in Canada

 960286

Program Ready II is dedicated to my mothers:

Minnie Nelson Brace Bourne,
who gave me birth, who loved and nurtured
me for forty years;

and

Isabel Murray MacNeill,
who took me into her family and has been a gracious
mother-in-law for almost the same length of time.

CONTENTS

INTRODUCTION

This is the fourth time I have assembled a group of programs for use in church groups. The first two books, no longer available, were called Quick'n'Easy and Quick'n'Easy #2. They were modest efforts directed specifically at women's groups in the United Church of Canada. The third collection, called Program Ready was published by the United Church Publishing House in 1994. This second volume, *Program Ready II* is the result of a perceived need throughout the church for program material written in simple language and easily adaptable for any Christian group. The programs may be used to begin a meeting with a short devotion, or to explore a topic further through discussion.

Once again the topics are grouped seasonally, to make selection easier, to emphasize topics that relate to what is going on within the full faith community, and to provide some balance and variety. I have added a section called "Preparation" for those who wish to provide some additional interest to the program section.

For many creative people the material in this book will be just a starting point. Add your own ideas, change the hymns, expand the information from other sources. The most heartening response I have received from users of the first *Program Ready* is from people who write to say that they used an idea from the book and built upon it, for a regional meeting, or perhaps a retreat. Others write to say that they added costumes to a playlet or skit they found in the book, or admitted that they only used the worship section because their group was not used to discussion in their meetings. This material is a *resource* and provides only a portion of the materials for worship, study and action that should be found in any faith community. I hope readers will find much usable material, yet not expect that all of the programs will be appropriate for any one group.

I would like to thank all who have provided ideas and suggestions for these programs. In particular I owe a great deal to my partner, Kenley, for his continual support and encouragement and his unerring ability to come up with appropriate scripture passages. Marlyne Myles and Joan Branscomb have provided continual moral support. Special thanks to Connie Corkum, Annette Keuning and Ken Shepard who agreed to read the draft manuscript; their comments and corrections helped me prepare for publication. I also thank the many United Church Women who responded to my request for suggestions, including those who attended the National Consultation at Burry Heights in Newfoundland in 1995. Thanks also to my editor, Ruth Bradley-St-Cyr, for her work on this project, particularly the Christmas and Babies program.

Dorothy MacNeill
Truro, Nova Scotia
November 15, 1996

Fall

1

Happy New Year in September

PREPARATION

Begin your new program year with a bang! Plan a New Year's Party, complete with balloons, streamers and noisemakers. Ask all members who plan to return to the group after your summer break to bring along a friend. Arrange for any guests to be introduced. Use name tags if appropriate. Make sure the time and date are advertised and get a phone tree going to ensure that everyone knows that things are starting up again.

A flip chart would be helpful for the program section.

WORSHIP

Call to Worship

Welcome! During the summer break we have worshipped God in different places and different ways. We do believe, however, that God is pleased to see us back in community, full of enthusiasm and energy, recreated and renewed and ready to seek

God's will for us in the days ahead. Let us begin with thanksgiving for the rest and relaxation of the summer days.

Prayer

The summer days seem to fly by, O God, and we thank you for them. We thank you for family and friends, for new places and familiar retreats. We thank you for warmth and colour and beauty. We pray for those who were unable to enjoy such things because of their economic situation or health concerns. We pray they were still aware of your presence in their lives, sensing your love through the summer sun, penetrating hospital walls and the tiniest windows of our homes. Give us joy in one another as we gather together once again, to seek your will and purpose for our group in this place, at this time. In the name of Jesus, the Christ, we pray. Amen.

Hymn

"Jesus, united by your grace"

Scripture

Acts 2:43-47

REFLECTION

It is not likely that members of the early Christian Church took an annual vacation. They were meeting together regularly, sharing all they had, and praising God continually. Such stories from the New Testament can leave us feeling guilty when we take a break from church activities from late May until early September. We need to remember, however, the difference between the lifestyles of those early Christians and our own. Their religion was brand new; ours is centuries old. The activities of daily living in those early years consumed most of everyone's time and energy. Water had to be carried, crops had to be tended, everything was made by hand or not made at all. We cannot possibly compare our lifestyles to theirs, nor should we try. What we do need to compare, however, is the faith that eventually led many of those early Christians into lion's dens or the catacombs, to the faith that modern people often put into one hour a week, with maybe a committee or small group meeting once a month.

But we are here to celebrate! We are beginning a new year of activity. We will be doing some things that we have done in years past; we may be contemplating a change in others. The whole church year lies ahead of us, beginning with Advent and Christmas, on to Epiphany and Lent, then the glorious Easter season and the thrill of Pentecost. Many opportunities await us, both within our faith community and in outreach activities to the community and world around us.

In generating enthusiasm there is one danger of which we need to be aware. Some may recognize the old saying, "Never bite off more than you can chew!" In modern terms it's called burnout. There may be a need to say "no" occasionally as we begin to get excited about the year's work. There will certainly be a need to make decisions about how much we can do. We must determine our priorities for the year, priorities that will be different for each of us.

But this is party time! We're happy to be here, let's have some fun!

PROGRAM

Share some of your summer activities. One way to do this if a group is large is to form two equal circles, one inside the other. Have one circle walk clockwise, the other counter-clockwise, at a given signal they share their most enjoyable summer activity with the person opposite them in the other circle. Do this three or four times, using topics like the worst thing that happened this summer, or the funniest. In a smaller group, simply sharing and catching up with one another would be sufficient.

Then, dream some dreams. Have group members talk in pairs about the most challenging thing you might consider doing this coming year. Encourage people to be daring, to stretch their imaginations. Some pairs might think it would be nice to build a low-income housing project; others might come up with ideas like a massive stewardship campaign that would eliminate all the smaller fund-raising projects; or an adopt-a-grandparent program. The sky is the limit for dreams.

If possible, list the dreams on a flip chart. In any brainstorming session it is important to accept all ideas without judgment. Something that sounds outrageous at first may spark other, more realistic ideas. After listing all ideas, go back and weed out the unworkable ones, and then look carefully at those that are left to see if you could possibly make one or two of the dreams come true.

There may be local projects that need discussion at this time of year. It's a good time to reassure people that they don't have to try to do everything but encourage them to support the group's activities to whatever extent seems appropriate. Remember it is the fear of having to say "no" to being asked to do too much that often prevents people from participating at all.

CLOSING

Make sure that any guests present feel comfortable in your group, and invite them to return soon.

2

Growing Old Gracefully

PREPARATION

This program could be used as a birthday celebration, or any time that a group of seniors wants to celebrate their status. Birthday cards or a birthday cake could be shared at the close. Or, the program could be used with a seniors' group towards the end of the year, when a small calendar would be a nice closing gift.

For use during the program, prepare one nicely wrapped gift containing something that can be shared. Depending on the number in your group, this could be small packages of facial tissues, candy or cookies, napkins or coasters. A larger gathering might be able to use this idea if members are sitting in table groups, then one gift would need to be prepared for each of the number of table groups expected.

WORSHIP

Call to Worship

"...those who wait for the Lord shall renew their strength, they shall mount up with wings like eagles, they shall run and not be weary, they shall walk and not faint." (Isaiah 40:31) Let us wait upon the Lord as we worship together. Let us pray:

Prayer

God of all our years, God of all grace, we do get weary sometimes, and younger people run and walk much faster than we do. Grant us the ability to enjoy the benefits of growing older without wishing for renewed youth. Give us instead, we pray, renewed interest in all that is going on around us, renewed enthusiasm for the activities we are able to enjoy, and a new appreciation of the world around us. Make our time together an opportunity to gain a new awareness of your gift of grace. In Jesus' name we pray, Amen.

Hymn

"Amazing Grace"

Scripture

Ephesians 1:1-14 (Emphasize the word *grace* whenever it appears.)

REFLECTION

The word *grace* is probably the most difficult word in the English vocabulary to define. Webster's Compact Dictionary uses a variety of words to describe it: charm, attractiveness; easy and refined motion, manners, etc.; ornament, accomplishment; favour; divine favour; short thanksgiving before or after a meal; title of a duke or archbishop. To grow old gracefully, then, is to exhibit some of these qualities in our lives. Older people who retain their charm and attractiveness are a joy to see; those who retain the ability to move around with an easy and refined motion are truly blessed. None would want to be considered an ornament, but most would be pleased to be told that their lives represented some sort of real accomplishment, other than simply growing old. Growing old while being favored by God is truly something to which we can all aspire.

Favored by God doesn't mean that we have led a life free of trouble and pain and disappointment. It means that throughout all of our lives, God has been with us. Just that. Those who grow old gracefully have about them a calmness that takes one day at a time, with each day filled with the awareness that they are not alone. They may not be able to move arms and legs as easily as they would wish, but there is a smile on their faces, or in their eyes.

A young woman once wrote a letter to herself, to be read when she reached senior citizen status. In it she tried to indicate some of the things that seniors sometimes do that make them seem less than graceful — things like expecting people to enjoy repeated stories; talking more than listening; interfering in their children's lives. She hoped that as a senior she would still enjoy reading and travelling, but she wanted to remember that her grandmother always wanted to go wherever her son and daughter-in-law went, and that was not always a good idea! She wanted her children to know that if she were ever completely bedridden by a stroke, she would like to have stuffed animals around her (especially her teddies) and she would like to be able to hear classical music, played softly.

We all grow old by the grace of God. We have no control over our years. Accidents and disease are part of living. Why they strike one person and not another is not ours to know. Growing old gracefully, however, is possible for all of us, whether we live for two more weeks, or twenty more years. Because God's grace is a free gift, if we reach out and take the gift, open it, and enjoy it, that grace will be evident in our lives.

Prayer

Eternal God, you make all things new and yet you are always the same. Grant that as we go forward in faith, we may continue to live in your divine favour. Guide us in all our doings, and guard all our days, so that we may spend our lives in your service. And finally, by your grace, may we attain the glory of everlasting life; through Jesus Christ our Lord. Amen.

PROGRAM

Some discussion on aging could center around questions such as the following:

- Do you know someone who has grown old gracefully? How does that grace show itself?
- Can anyone remember wanting, as a young adult, to age like someone they admired — only to discover that the person was not as old as they thought?
- Which birthday was most significant or memorable for you? What made that particular birthday special?
- Would anyone like to describe what they understand about the grace of God?
- Most references to grace in the Bible are in benedictions, such as, "the grace of our Lord Jesus Christ be with all of you." Is there any difference between the grace of God and the grace of Jesus?
- Does saying grace at meals detract from the deeper meaning of God's grace?

Place the wrapped gift before the group and explain that there is only one package, but someone has to take it and open it. Spend a few minutes talking about what might be in the gift — what would they like to receive? **Do not let someone pick it up and give it to another!** This may take some time, but ask people to share their feelings about why they do not want to reach out for the gift. When someone finally takes the gift, ask them why they decided to do it, and ask the others how they feel now that someone has taken what could have been theirs.

Is there another free gift available to us? (God's grace and God's love.) Have the person who took the gift open it up, and hopefully she/he will be aware that the gift can be shared. So can grace!

CLOSING

The grace of the Lord Jesus Christ, the love of God, and the communion of the Holy Spirit be with all of you.

3

Teach Us How to Pray

PREPARATION

In your regular prayer time ask God to help your group to talk freely about prayer. Pray that you will be able to lead the members into an increased understanding of prayer.

If you wish, photocopy the information sheet on prayer for distribution at your meeting.

Check with your local Bible book store for short prayers on wallet size cards, or on bookmarks. If your budget permits, purchase one for each member. Or make some of your own.

WORSHIP

Call to Worship

Moses taught that God required people to make a daily animal sacrifice, to claim forgiveness and to indicate their desire to please God. (Lev 6:8-13) Before teaching the disciples the prayer that we call The Lord's Prayer, Jesus simply said, "This, then, is how you should pray:" Let us begin our worship by repeating that prayer together:

Prayer

Our Father, who art in heaven, hallowed by thy name. Thy kingdom come, thy will be done on earth, as it is in heaven. Give us this day our daily bread and forgive us our trespasses as we forgive those who trespass against us. And lead us not into temptation, but deliver us from evil, for thine is the kingdom and the power and the glory. For ever and ever. Amen.

Hymn

"Sweet hour of prayer" or "What a friend we have in Jesus"

Scripture

Matthew 6:5-15

REFLECTION

Many of us are familiar with the opening words of a poem about prayer by James Montgomery — "Prayer is the soul's sincere desire, unuttered or expressed...."[1] It has always provided a neat excuse for those of us who find it difficult to actually verbalize our prayers. We tell ourselves that God knows what we are thinking and that we don't really need to use words. And although there is no doubt that we can have a personal communion with God that is quite wordless, it doesn't often happen when we are working, or socializing, or watching T.V. During meditation, which requires that we block out of our minds all that is distracting us, we concentrate on emptying the mind of everything except the one thing we wish to focus upon. In prayer, that focus would be God.

There is another type of prayer that doesn't require our spoken words. We can talk to God as we go about our daily routine, offering our praise for the beautiful world in which we live, sharing our joys and sorrows, mentioning people by name who need special prayers, and asking for guidance for ourselves. Watering plants that remind us of certain people, possibly because we received them as a gift from that person, can provide an opportunity to bring their names to God in prayer. There are words involved, but God is the only one who needs to hear them.

At other times, however, there is a need for us to use spoken words of prayer within our faith community. This may happen during those times of worship when there is no particular person present who has been set apart for ministry. In many congregations lay people participate in regular worship by reading scripture. Increasingly they are being asked to lead in prayer. Reading prayers or other devotional material written by someone else can be helpful on such occasions, as long as we don't become dependent on them. These things are supplements to our prayers, not a substitute. When used thoughtlessly even the beautiful prayer that Jesus taught can be meaningless.

Some people are always ready to pray aloud. Some do so fluently and they are able to give those who hear a feeling of communion with God. Others may pray using words that have been memorized and the same phrases are sometimes repeated over and over again. Such prayers can be especially meaningful in a familiar setting. Some contemporary prayers have value for their freshness and startling images. It is always the spirit of prayer that is important, not the words.

Sometimes when we are standing with someone who is having a difficult time we wish that we could offer to pray with them. Like the disciples, we wish that someone could teach us how to pray. No doubt the disciples used the prayer that Jesus taught them on many occasions, but if that was the only prayer they used we would not have the rich prayers of the early church to inspire us, as the tradition of praying in our own words would never have started. We can learn to pray by praying. We can learn to make our prayers personal and relevant. Such prayers bring all who hear into the very presence of God.

Prayer

God of all our prayers, your son urged us to be perfect, yet he accepted and loved everyone he met. Accept our imperfections and guide us along the path of learning how to pray. Help us to be open with one another and willing to share our faith. Give us the confidence we need to lead others in prayer, to speak boldly to you, knowing that you hear every word we say, you know every desire of our hearts. Amen.

PROGRAM

Begin by sharing stories about prayers learned in childhood. Follow this by asking how people feel when they are asked to lead in prayer. Are there people in your group who do this quite readily? If so, ask them if they can explain when they first started doing this and why it comes easily to them when it is often very difficult for other people.

Discuss the pros and cons of reading prayers written by other people.

If you have prepared copies of the prayer information sheet, pass them out now and allow some time for people to read them. There may or may not be discussion on these, depending on the experience of your group.

We assume that prayer is something that comes naturally, that it is only necessary to teach prayer to children and that practice is not required. So it is that many adults find themselves knowing the Lord's Prayer, and possibly some prayers for grace before meals or childhood bedtime prayers. Very few adults are willing to pray in public, unless the prayer is in a written form, most often written by someone else. A Japanese missionary to Canada in the 70's wondered why Canadians always seemed to pray from a piece of paper, instead of from their heart. Those he asked had no satisfying answer for him.

One way to practice prayer is to have a circle of prayer during your group meeting. At first members may be more comfortable if they keep their eyes open. As they gain experience they may wish to close their eyes and hold the hand of the person next to them.

To begin your prayer circle, suggest a topic. Probably the easiest to begin with is thanksgiving. Ask each person to express a thanksgiving thought in a sentence. Each sentence should begin with the words, "Thank you God, for..." rather than allowing people to just name something for which they are thankful. Allow people to pass by simply saying the words, "thank you..." If you wish to hold hands, passing can be signaled to the next person in the circle with a slight pressure of the hand.

One prayer circle does not qualify as enough practice to become proficient in prayer. Repeat the process, using intercession as a topic. This time ask members to use these words:

"I lift to your light (name of a person or persons) who (specific situation) that (he/she/they) may (your hope or desire for them.)"

An example of this would be: "I lift to your light my friend Jane who has just learned of the death of her mother, that she may find comfort and support in her time of grief." Another example: "I lift to your light the hungry children of our world, that they may know that many people want to help them." If your group is quite inexperienced, you may need to explain this format quite carefully and be prepared for some to pass.

Discuss the possibility of using prayer circles during some of your regular meetings.

CLOSING

Close with a prayer that lifts up what your group has experienced during the program. If you, as leader, are uncomfortable with this, ask well in advance for someone else to do it for you.

1   James Montgomery, "Prayer is the soul's sincere desire," *Anglican Hymn Book* #603.

4

Remembering

PREPARATION

Blow up a balloon — red would be most suitable — and write on it with a soft marker the words, "I remember..."

WORSHIP

Call to Worship

Remembering is always in season, but in November there are two special days that remind us to remember. November 11th is Remembrance Day in Canada, when we wear red poppies to help us remember the sacrifices made by men and women who have fought for our country in times of war. For the Christian Church all over the world, the first Sunday in November is called All Saints Day, a day when we remember those whom we have known and loved and who are no longer with us. Let us begin our worship and our remembering with prayer:

Prayer

We thank you, God, for the gift of memory. Sometimes we forget things that we should remember, like where we put our glasses or our car keys, or whether there's enough milk for breakfast. And we confess that sometimes we remember things that we wish we could forget, like a call we didn't make, or an unkind word spoken in anger. We gather in faith communities so that we can remember your love for us, and how you showed us that love through the life of your son, Jesus. We acknowledge your presence with us now, through his spirit. Amen.

Our memories may fail us, but it is good to know that God will never forsake us — or forget us. Let us sing together:

Hymn
"I will never forget you, my people"

Scripture
Luke 22:14-20

REFLECTION

The Feast of the Passover is an important event in the life of all Jews. It has been important since the historic exodus from Egypt, when Moses led the slaves out of Egypt. While they were preparing to flee they were instructed to make a mark with blood from the family sacrificial lamb on the door post of their homes so that the angel of death would pass over their house during the night. They left their homes so quickly that the bread they carried with them hadn't time to rise, so the re-enactment of the Passover always involves unleavened bread, and wine to represent the blood on the door post.

Jesus celebrated Passover, and because of the last Passover meal that he shared with his followers before his crucifixion, the Passover has become for Christians a way to remember Jesus. We call our remembering Holy Communion, the Lord's Supper, or the Eucharist, and we eat bread and drink wine because of the instructions given in First Corinthians, when Jesus said, "This is my body that is broken for you. Do this in remembrance of me." Engraved on communion tables all over the world are those words, "In remembrance of me."

These words may seem very familiar, but for many in our society today they mean nothing. They have no Christian memory. They have never attended church or Sunday School, nor have their parents. Their memory of the Bible comes only from secular references, or through hearing the name of God and Jesus used as swear words. Some people who attend church regularly lack a basic understanding of what is in the Bible or how it came to be written and compiled. We all remember Bible verses that we have heard sung, or — if we're lucky — verses that we memorized in Sunday School. We find it difficult to locate specific Bible stories, or even incidents in the life of Jesus, without looking them up in a reference book.

Every day of our lives we are creating memories. As we grow older we are surprised by what other people remember about us. Maybe we said or did something that we have long forgotten, but the person on the other end of a thoughtful gesture or a kind word may remember it always. Children seem to remember things that their parents are sure never happened.

The gift of memory gives us the joy of being able to remember the good things of life and the ability to forget some of the mundane, or bad things. This is called selective memory. Memory helps us learn to look after ourselves. If we get sick eating roast pork, remembering should help us choose something else next time. A child remembers the pain of touching something hot and obeys instructions to not touch next time. Usually. The loss of memory is one of the saddest afflictions that can overtake these rather delicate bodies of ours.

And so we remember. We remember war veterans, people who have gone on before us, the pleasant days of our childhood, and we remember our Christian heritage. Let us also remember to create new memories, to make sure that those around us know what our values and beliefs are, and to pass on the history of our own families to the younger generation. What will our friends remember about us when we die? We may not consider that very important at this point, but many believe that being remembered is our immortality. The important memory for Christians to keep alive, however, is the gospel message. It is our obligation to live the good news of the gospel in our communities, in our country, in our world.

Prayer

As we remember, O God, help us to give special attention to the memories of our Christian heritage. Help us to cherish the values that are important to us and to share stories of our faith journey with those around us. In memory of your Son, and in his name we pray. Amen.

PROGRAM

Share some memories. The leader should bring out the balloon, with the words, "I remember" written on it, and hold it while she shares her earliest memory. Then she passes the balloon to another person who does the same. Depending on the size of your group, allow four or five people to share a memory. Then do the same with the following suggestions, or make up your own:

- your first memory of church or Sunday School
- your favourite teacher, in Sunday School or regular school
- memories or stories from parents or grandparents regarding war

Following this, give members of the group an opportunity to share some things they do especially to create memories. Ask the question, "what in your home do you *always* do, that you think your family and friends will always remember?"

Ask if anyone would like to share what they would like people to remember about them.

What can this group do to help your faith community in its task of passing on the heritage of our Christian faith?

Closing

Make a memory. Some suggestions: take a picture of your group; serve something outrageous instead of your standard refreshments; tell members that whenever they see a knife on its edge in the future, they will remember your current leader; or come up with your own ideas.

Advent

5

Journey to Christmas #1

PREPARATION

Prepare an Advent calendar for each person expected.
You may photocopy the December page of a current calendar, or be creative and make your own.

WORSHIP

Call to Worship

Everyone, then, went to register, each to their own home town.
Joseph and Mary went from the town of Nazareth in Galilee to the
town of Bethlehem in Judea. As we begin our journey to Bethlehem, let us prepare ourselves by gathering together the important things that we want to take with us. Let us begin with prayer:

Prayer

God of the traveler, you seek those who are willing to venture
forth into unknown places. You ask us to trust, and you promise
to travel with us. As we journey to Christmas this year, we want
to take with us the practice of prayer. We will need your help, for
in the busyness of our lives we often forget to pray. Accept our

sincere desires, unuttered or expressed, and fill us with the confidence of your continued presence and love. Amen.

Hymn
"Lord Jesus, of you I will sing"

Scripture
Luke 2:1-5a

REFLECTION

Faith journey is an expression that may have been somewhat overworked in recent years. We know that we travel through life, from birth to death, and that our faith grows and changes along the way. It is important to recognize this process, and important to share some parts of our journey with others. Calling this process a journey reminds us of the lives of many who have gone before us: The Exodus, when Moses led his people out of slavery, is a journey that has been central in the Judeo/Christian heritage. The journeys of Paul began the missionary history of our faith. Jesus' final journey into Jerusalem, as well as his birth in Bethlehem and his travelling ministry throughout the area of Galilee, are all integral to the gospel story.

The church has designated the four weeks prior to Christmas as a time of preparation. We call it Advent, the time of waiting. It is a time to think about our journey to Christmas. Too often we begin our Christmas celebrations well in advance of December 25th and many of these activities are not within our control. We live in a world where Christmas decorations sometimes precede Halloween. Our social obligations around the Christmas season need much pre-planning and work. There are many things we cannot influence at this time of year, but we can control how we plan our own lives during this time period. We can learn to allow time for the things that are most important to us. We can learn to say a gentle "no" to things that we do not consider essential and we can include some special activities that are especially meaningful for ourselves and those around us. These are individual decisions, what feels right for one person may not suit another.

There is a story told of some travelers who were together on a train on Christmas Eve. This is a unique day on our calendar, for on this day people smile at one another, people talk to one another, people share parts of themselves with one another. So it was with the train travelers. They told stories, they shared memories of Christmases past, they laughed and joked, trying to make the most of the fact that they were not where they wanted to be on this special night. Finally one person said, "I'd like to read a story. I think it is the very best Christmas story in the world." He took out a book and began the famous tale that begins, "Marley was dead..." Everyone listened as the gifted story teller read the familiar words. Then another traveler spoke up in response. "I love that story, but I have to disagree with you when you say it is the very best Christmas story. Let me read that one for you." And he opened his Bible and read the Christmas story from the gospel of Luke.

Take the *real* Christmas story with you as you travel towards Christmas this year. It will help you to remember why we celebrate on December 25th.

Prayer
God of Christmas and of all our days, we thank you for the gift of your Son, for his life, which gives us an example to follow, and for his death and resurrection, which give us the strength we need to live out our own faith journey. We thank you for the gift of the Spirit, for the knowledge that we are never alone, no matter where our journeys take us. In quietness and confidence we travel on. Amen.

PROGRAM

Christmas is a time for fun! If your group enjoys games, play the familiar Packing My Suitcase game only vary it to fit the Advent journey. The first person to play says, "I'm making a journey to Christmas and I'm taking an attitude of .... (e.g. prayer.)" The next person says, "I'm making a journey to Christmas and I'm taking an attitude of prayer and ... (praise?)" The third person repeats the sentence, adding his/her own attitude.

Note: This game is only appropriate for a group of approximately six to twelve, since the last person has to try and remember *all* of the attitudes. (Some other suggestions are grace, kindness, forgiveness, cheerfulness, thrift, etc.)

The leader should write down, for her own use, the attitudes mentioned during the game. Then, when the game is over, discuss how each attitude could influence our journey to Christmas. Ask group members to give illustrations of the attitudes as the discussion progresses. If you do not wish to play the game, make your own list of attitudes to use in the discussion.

Most journeys cannot be called uneventful — we take a wrong turn, there is a construction detour, someone gets sick, or we run out of gas. What are some of the problems or roadblocks that pop up as we begin our journey to Christmas? (We run out of energy or get tired quite often, we set unrealistic objectives, there may be illness, unhappy memories, or even tragedy.) Discuss these, and have people share some personal experiences of various hazards they have encountered on the road to Christmas in years past.

Finally, discuss whether or not the attitudes you talked about earlier will help when we encounter some of these problems. What does the group consider the most important attitude to take on the journey to Christmas?

CLOSING

If you have prepared an Advent calendar give one to each person present. Tell them that there are three important things to put on their Advent calendars: time for God, time for reaching out to someone, and time for the care of their own spirituality.

6

Journey to Christmas #2

PREPARATION

There are many environmental agencies that produce helpful booklets and pamphlets containing various suggestions and ideas for celebrating Christmas in an environmentally-friendly way. Locate some of these to display or to give to members at the close of your program.

Some books that may help are *Unplug the Christmas Machine: A Complete Guide to Putting Love and Joy Back into the Season*, by Jo Robinson and Jean C. Staeheli (New York: William Morrow and Co., 1991); *Fifty-two Simple Ways to Make Christmas Special*, by Jan Dargatz (Nashville: Thomas Nelson, 1991); and *Treasury of Celebrations*, by Carolyn Pogue (Winfield, B.C.: Northstone, 1996).

If you use the suggested closing, you will need to recycle some old Christmas cards, one for each person expected.

WORSHIP

Call to Worship

Although Herod asked the Magi to come back and give him news of the Messiah they were seeking, they were warned in a dream not to do so. They took an alternate route back to their homes. As we travel towards Christmas during this Advent season is it possible that we too should seek an alternate route? Let us worship God, who convinced the Magi to change direction, and who is still willing to guide those who question the well trodden path.

Prayer

God of tradition and heritage, God of innovation and change, we value all that we have enjoyed about Christmas celebrations in the past, but we want to find new ways to rejoice over the birth of your Son. We want to find ways to keep the best of what has gone before and still reach out for freshness and renewed thanksgiving. Above all, we want to enjoy our celebrations without endangering any of your creation. Amen.

Hymn

"To show by touch and word"

Scripture

Matthew 2:11-14

REFLECTION

It was not only the Magi who took an alternate route away from the Bethlehem manger. Mary and Joseph did not return to their home in Nazareth. Instead, they fled to Egypt. We do not know what happened to the Holy Family in Egypt, because there is only one story in the Bible that tells us anything about Jesus between his birth and the beginning of his ministry. That is in the gospel of Luke, when Jesus was twelve, and apparently the family once again lived in Nazareth.

Since the Bible is full of stories of various journeys, we can find other examples of people who took alternate routes. Jonah didn't want to travel where God was leading him at all, and his alternate route ended up in the belly of a whale. Joseph was quite happy in the land of Canaan but due to his jealous brothers he ended up in Egypt against his will. And the most famous alternate route in the New Testament follows Paul's memorable journey to Damascus. After his conversion, Paul was happy preaching in Damascus, but his alternate route took him back to Jerusalem and into fierce opposition.

There are people today who take alternate routes in life. There are those who give up good careers to become trained for ordered ministry. There are mothers who choose to stay at home with their children, in spite of a lowered standard of living because they receive no pay for their work. There are others who return to school and university as mature students, seeking either improved opportunities for work, or their own enrichment.

What are some of the alternate routes to Christmas? As we begin to make preparations for December 25th, are there things that we can do differently to make the time before Christmas more meaningful, for ourselves and for those around us? What is it that prevents us from saying "no" to traditions that are empty and without connection to the real meaning of Christ's birth? What prevents us from starting new traditions?

Part of the reason is that traditions are important to us. They remind us of our heritage, and, like antiques, their value increases the older they get. The problem is, there may be too many of them! We find ourselves caught up in carrot puddings and fruit cakes that we've learned are *not* part of a healthy diet. We put more lights on our house this year perhaps because a neighbour had more than we did last year, so our power bill goes up, as does our drain on the environment. We give a gift because we received one last year, and we make sure that the gift is comparable to the one we received. And on it goes.

We are the only ones who can put a detour sign on our road to Christmas. We are the only ones who can decide what is the most important item on our agenda during the weeks of Advent. We can be prodded and reminded of the true meaning of Christmas each time we light an Advent candle in church, but we are also being continually influenced by society around us. If we are to find an alternate route to Christmas it has to be our own decision.

PROGRAM

There is nothing new about attempting to find alternate ways to celebrate Christmas. Start the program by having members of the group share some changes they have instigated in their own Christmas celebrations. Ask if these changes have been added on to what they already do traditionally, or if they have replaced something that has been a tradition for them.

Talk about the difference between Christmas in a home with small children and a home where there are no children, or where the children have grown up and moved away. Discover how many of your group actually have the kind of Christmas we see in T.V. commercials — Mom, Dad, the children, grandparents, aunts and uncles and friends, all having a wonderful time eating, drinking in a beautifully decorated house. Does this stereotypical Christmas affect us in any particular ways?

Share ideas for an environmentally friendly Christmas. If you have been able to obtain pamphlets or booklets, they could be used for this part of the program. If not, consider such things as:

- artificial or live Christmas trees
- trees that have not been chemically sprayed
- alternate ways of wrapping gifts
- consumable gifts
- recycle gift wrap and cardboard
- newer types of lighting, using less electricity

As well as being environmentally friendly, another alternate route to Christmas could involve actually *doing* something different that gives meaning to the celebrations. Discuss such things as:

- sharing Christmas dinner with some of the homeless people in our cities
- taking a small gift to some people who find themselves always working on Christmas day (Mom and Pop stores, maybe)
- going skiing or sledding instead of having a big Christmas dinner
- recycling last year's Christmas cards, by returning them to the one who sent them to you, with a friendly note

CLOSING

Distribute any pamphlets you may have collected, and/or recycle some Christmas cards: give one picture to each person and ask them to answer the following question on the back of the card: What will be on your alternate route to Christmas this year? Have them take the card home and place it on their fridge as a reminder.

7

Christmas and Babies

PREPARATION

This program is designed as a worship service. It is not the traditional feel-good Christmas service, however. Many people feel depressed for various reasons at this time of year and may appreciate a dose of realism to counteract the rosy nostalgia that is prevalent at holiday time.

If fire regulations permit, and if so desired, provide individual candles for each person expected. There should be a central Christ candle lit before the service and five other candles for the candle lighting part of the service.

You will need a worship center, consisting of a simple manger, a padded box or doll's crib. Also, two chairs, rocking chairs if possible, one at each side of your worship center. A dramatic effect would be achieved if spot lights could shine on these chairs alternately, as different characters are seated in them during the worship period, or a lamp could be placed beside each chair and the characters could turn them on as they take their places and turn them off as they leave.

WORSHIP

Call to Worship

You shall find a child, wrapped in bands of cloth and lying in a manger. Let us worship before the empty cradle where the central character in the Christmas drama will soon appear.

Hymn

"Come, thou long-expected Jesus"

Prayer

Empty cradles fill us with sadness, God. The Bible tells us that your people were walking in darkness before the coming of Jesus, the Light of the World. So then, the joy of his coming must have thrilled all who knew of it, just as the arrival of new babies usually fills our lives with love and happiness. As we think of cradles tonight, as we try to visualize the babies of our world, keep us mindful of the baby whose birth we celebrate, the baby who was born in a stable, the one who grew to be the Messiah, the Christ, Emmanuel, God with us. It is in his name we pray, Amen.

Scripture

Luke 1:26-38

1st Rocking Chair Story

Yes, the cradle is empty. I am a childless woman, envied by mothers coping with too many children, pitied by those who think no woman is complete unless she has produced a child of her own. But God does not pity me, or think me unfulfilled. God gives us all choices and sometimes one choice means that another cannot be made. That's the way life is and we often don't realize what effect some of our decisions will have later in life. But having made them, we live with them, just as I am living without children of my own.

My sister and brother both have kids and I baby-sit often, sometimes for a week at a time. The kids and the parents are both happy for the break from each other. And I have a great time too, taking them places I'd never go otherwise, like the zoo and the playground. My life is good, I have a strong identity through my family, my work, my hobbies, my friends; through what I do with my life rather than who I live with. I can say, like God, that I am who I am.

2nd Rocking Chair Story

Sometimes I've wished my cradle was empty. This is the fifth baby I've rocked to sleep in this old rocking chair. But I love my children. That's why I left my husband. I'm on welfare now so lots of people think I'm a bum and should get a job instead, as if raising five kids isn't a job! When they see a woman with five kids on welfare they just assume I keep having kids so I can live off the system. But they don't know; they shouldn't judge.

I lived with that drunken man for years. He hit me, not too often at first, but after a while it was pretty well every week. Still, I thought my kids needed a father, even a bad one, until he started hitting them too. That's when I left. He kicked me in the stomach when I was pregnant with this one. Thank God she came out okay. The single woman talked about the choices she made, well, I had to make some too, and as she says, "That's how it is!" Some day these children will be grown, hopefully they won't be too screwed up. Some day I'll go back to school and go out and find work — it's those some-day dreams that keep me going, you know.

Hymn

"Gentle Mary laid her child"

3rd Rocking Chair Story

Our country was so beautiful before the war. Now nobody wants to come here, everybody wants to leave. I didn't want to have a baby in the middle of a war, but sometimes it happens. My husband and I were trying to be careful, we used to use birth control, but all the systems of normal life have broken down. No running water, no heat, no buses, no food, no medicine... no birth control. Still we were happy about the baby. He's our first. And then my husband got taken away somewhere. I don't know where he is or if I'll ever see him again.

It hasn't been easy. Thank God babies have mother's milk to sustain them. I couldn't make formula even if I wanted to with no clean water and no electricity. One of my friends tried formula, thinking that she was too underfed herself to feed a baby too. But her little girl got very sick and died. We have nothing to rely on here except ourselves. I'm getting my boy out of this country as soon as I can. I don't want to raise another soldier.

4th Rocking Chair Story

It was hard telling people I was pregnant. I wouldn't have had to if I'd had an abortion. No one would ever have known how stupid I acted. I fell for this guy, really hard. I was so swept away I forgot about birth control. Maybe part of me wanted to get pregnant because I wanted a part of him. I wanted us to be together. But he didn't want that.

I thought about abortion. I guess anyone would in my situation. But then I thought of all those couples out there who want babies so badly but can't have them. Practically nobody gives up their baby for adoption anymore. One of my friends said, "It will be too hard to give up the baby, why don't you just have an abortion?" But that didn't make any sense to me. Every child should be a wanted child and I know someone out there wants this one so badly that she cries herself to sleep a lot. I do too, wishing things could be different, but my faith and my real friends have helped sustain me. I can't give my baby a home or a father, but I gave her life. Her new parents will pick her up in a couple of days. I almost can't bear the thought of giving her up, now that I've actually met her, but I've met her new parents too and I know they'll give her the home that she needs. I hope I'll have a family some day too.

Hymn

"Away in a manger"

5th Rocking Chair Story

I'm married and we have one little boy who is four, and now this baby girl. I thank God every day for them. I've had sort of a hard time having children. Two miscarriages, lots of pregnancy problems, and both delivered by cesarean. In spite of all that I wanted more children but my husband went and had a vasectomy. He said he didn't want to see me suffer any more. I know he means well...

I'm staying at home with the kids for as long as I can. There aren't many other moms around the neighbourhood these days, but some of the nannies are nice. It's hard work to find peer support for me and other kids for mine to play with. We certainly miss my income and had to scale back our finances pretty severely. That second income wasn't paying for extras, it was paying our mortgage. We renegotiated that and finally paid off the car before the baby came. I think we will name her Joy, since she was born so close to Christmas.

6th Rocking Chair Story

My name is Mary. My baby is reborn every Christmas because so many people celebrate his birth. They call it a miracle now, and it was. But every mother knows her baby is a miracle too. All children are children of God. Having my baby in that time and place was very dangerous. I was very frightened for myself and the child I was carrying. Joseph could have shunned me. My family could have disowned me. I could have been stoned for adultery. But Joseph was also touched by God. He protected us, loved us, found us safety and shelter time and again.

We never had much to live on but we had enough for all our children. Plenty of love, anyway. We always thought that Jesus was special. I even believed that God would speak through him one day, but I didn't know he would have to die so young for it. That broke my heart. There was a war on then too. A battle that's still being fought. A war between love and hate. When he died I thought hate had won. But if it really had the name of my son would be unknown these days. Love returns to us in the birth of every child. If you want to remember the birth of Jesus, remember that every child should be welcomed into the world and allowed to grow in peace.

Hymn

"Hope for the children"

Candle Lighting

(Those who have told the Rocking Chair stories come forward together to light five candles from the Christ candle.)

Number 1

We light this candle and pray for women who, for any reason, have not borne children. May those who chose to be childless feel that their decision is accepted by those who know and love them. May those whose desire for children has not been fulfilled help love and care for other children. It takes a whole village to raise a child, not just parents.

Number 2

We light this candle and pray for women who have more children than they can care for. May they find support and care for themselves. May they find ways to break out of their cycle of violence, poverty, or despair. We pray for all those who try to assist and understand. Help us all to reach out a hand of friendship to help ease their burdens.

Number 3

We light this candle and pray for all victims of war: men, women and children. May those whose lives have been exploded in violence find the courage to continue to struggle for the freedom to live in peace. We pray especially for the children who are victims of war, "ethnic cleansing," famine, disaster, and violence throughout the world. We pray for peace keepers everywhere and their children back home.

Number 4

We light this candle and pray for all those who have the courage to bring children into this world, whether they will raise them or not. We pray for those who are faced with tough choices, whatever they decide to do. We pray for all those who try to assist and understand. Help us all to reach out a hand of friendship to help ease their burdens.

Number 5

We light this candle and pray for loving families throughout the world. May they give thanks for their blessings and seek opportunities to make life easier for others. We pray that one day all children will be born into loving families, that they will be loved and cared for, educated and trained, so that they may move our world into a time of peace and well-being for all.

Number 6

The central candle is our Christ candle. It was lit when we began, and it will remain lighted as we leave. Jesus Christ is the Prince of Peace, the Light of the World, the light that no darkness can extinguish. We celebrate Jesus' birth, but it is in the way we live our own lives that we honour his life.

Come then, light your candles as we lay the infant Jesus in the empty cradle and as we remember the children of our world.

(A real baby or doll is placed in the central crib and participants go forward to light individual candles, then circle the church and sing:)

Hymn

"Silent Night, Holy Night"

Benediction

We celebrate the birth of a baby, a child who grew up to say, "Let the children come unto me, for of such is the Kingdom of Heaven." As you go into Christmas, take note of the children around you, and see the celebrations, and the world, through their eyes.

May the blessing of God, our loving Parent, Jesus, the Prince of Peace, and the Spirit of gentleness go with you. Amen.

Epiphany

8

Epiphany Embers

PREPARATION

This is a program that really should take place around a fireplace. Comfortable chairs and subdued lighting will help to set the mood. If that is not possible, assemble an assortment of candles on a fireproof tray and place it where all can see the flames. (Be careful not to place a metal tray directly onto a wooden table, etc. Make sure to use a trivet or heat-absorbing pad to protect the table.)

WORSHIP

Call to Worship

Warmth and light are treasured elements of our lives. During Epiphany we think about the light of the star that led the Magi to the Christ Child, and we see their visit as a symbol of the showing forth of Jesus as the light of the whole world. Let us, then, worship the triune God: God who created the sun and stars, Jesus, who warmed the hearts of those who knew him, and the Holy Spirit, source of our confidence and comfort. Let us begin with a song about light:

Hymn
"I am the light of the world"

Scripture
John 1:1-9 and John 8:12

REFLECTION

During the Christmas season we have been surrounded by light. Candles, tree lights and spotlights are symbols not only of the winter solstice, the return of the sun, but they represent to us the fact that Jesus Christ is the Light of the World.

The season of Epiphany emphasizes light, beginning with the star, shining in the east. The visiting astrologers who followed that star were foreigners, suggesting the tiny baby born in Bethlehem was to become important to the whole world, not only the Messiah so longed for by the Jews. The visit of the Magi probably took place sometime after the actual birth. The Bible says they visited the child in a house, not a stable, and in the story of Herod's slaughter of the innocents it seems that Herod felt the child might be as old as two years, as he ordered all boys two and under to be slain.

There are many stories that revolve around the magic and fascination of light. One relates the tale of a prisoner of war who was saving a stub of candle as a last protection against starvation. He would nibble on it occasionally, but always hid it quickly so that fellow prisoners would not see it and expect to share it. Then, one of the men realized that it was Christmas Eve, and they began to talk of loved ones, telling stories of Christmases past, and sharing the hope that before next Christmas the war would be over. Finally, in the spirit of the season the prisoner decided to share his candle. Not to be eaten, but to be lit as a symbol of the birth of Jesus, the Light of the World. All the prisoners in that camp swear the candle burned all night long. The faith symbolized by the light maintained their bodies and spirits until the war really did end and they were released.

Another story is told of a woman who dreamed that she was standing before Jesus with a candle in her hand. Jesus lit her candle, but as she turned away from him to walk into the darkness her own breath blew the candle out. She returned to Jesus and he lit her candle again. But again it went out as soon as she began her journey into the darkness. This happened again and again, but in her dream she noticed one thing: each time her candle was re-lit she was able to travel a little farther into the dark unknown.

We may not be in a physical prison. We may not be forced to move into the dark places of our lives alone. Our prison may be our refusal to accept new ideas. Our darkness may be an unwillingness to become involved. Whatever our need, the Light is there for all through the continual presence of Jesus Christ, the Light of the World, the one who promised to be with his followers until the end of the age.

Prayer

Creator God, you brought light into the world at creation, you sent light into our darkness by offering your Son. We praise and thank you for the warmth of the sun and the life of Jesus, our Saviour. Forgive us when we fear the darkness of the unknown. Hold our hand as we venture forth. Give us the confidence to live as reflectors of the light of your Son, lighting up the darkness of our world. Amen.

PROGRAM

Focus the attention of group members on the fireplace, or the candles. Ask them to recollect memories of other fireplaces, or sources of warmth and light, in their lives. How was their home heated when they were children? Did anyone have a moving spiritual experience during a campfire at church camp? Does a fireplace remind them of someone they love?

Ask if anyone has ever experienced fire in a destructive way. Allow them to share this. Assuming that all people and pets were safe, what would they consider the most important thing to save if their house caught fire?

Fire is a cleansing agent, and can be compared to a prayer of confession. Ask if there are things in the past that people would like to lay on the fire as a symbol of something they regret, or would like to forget.

Move into a time of thanksgiving and intercessory prayer by quoting part of this old camp poem:

"Kneel always when you light a fire, kneel reverently and thankful be for God's unfailing charity. And on the ascending flame inspire a prayer..."

Allow people to contribute their prayers of thanksgiving, and to offer to God their concerns for certain people and situations.

CLOSING

The flames in the fireplace will die down. The candles will be extinguished. The flames have reminded us of many things as we have talked. Let them remind us once again that the light that came into the world with Jesus will never go out. The Light of the world is not a candle that we see in church or a person we read about in the Bible. It is the living presence of God, God with us, Immanuel. It is the reality of a God who has always been, who is now, and who will always be. Epiphany holds out the hope that God will one day be present to the whole world; it is a promise of peace, and justice, for all of God's people. The Light has come into the world and the darkness shall never put it out.

9

January Thaw

PREPARATION

You may need to change the name of this program if your geographical climate doesn't include a January thaw. Your winter experience may instead include a Chinook, or you may live somewhere that doesn't have this period of warm weather right in the middle of winter. Please adapt the material to suit your area.

Since a January thaw is a sort of serendipity event, you may wish to do something completely different from your usual routine during this meeting. Reverse the agenda, serve refreshments at a different time, have toasted bagels instead of your usual sandwiches and sweets. Anything that is a change will emphasize this change in the weather, and this may prompt some change within your group.

For the closing, sketch a butterfly and a caterpillar on a banner or poster with the words, "Change? Who, me?"

Reflection

We begin in the middle, with a reflection.

A January thaw brings welcome relief to folk in Nova Scotia. They enjoy the melting snow, even though they know more will arrive before Spring. For other people the thaw can bring devastating floods, strong winds, and they learn to fear this particular time of year. Most types of change are something like the January thaw — welcomed by some, feared by others. It also reminds us that while there are opportune times for change, often at regular points in our lives, sometimes unexpected windows open.

Think, for instance, of a family that faces an empty nest for the first time. This event is expected to happen eventually, but is always a surprise when it finally arrives. Being a couple again can provide an opportunity to evaluate, and possibly record family history, or to plan plans and dream dreams for the years to come.

Becoming a widow or widower, or going through a divorce, is not such a pleasant change, but once the grieving period is over we are given an opportunity once again to set a new direction, to open ourselves to new activities, and to new friends. Other such windows for change in our lives include moving to a new home, welcoming a new minister to our congregation, recovering from a major illness, or becoming either a care giver, or one who must learn to accept the care of others.

There are good changes and unpleasant changes, exciting changes and life-threatening changes. A certainty in being human is the reality of change. Our bodies change as we mature and then again as we grow old. Our attitudes change as we stretch our minds and read our Bibles and our newspapers. Listen to the words of St. Paul as he lists some of the things that affect our lives and as he expresses his confident faith that no change in our lives can separate us from God:

Worship

Scripture
Romans 8:35-39

Prayer
Eternal and ever loving God, we know that your love for us never changes. Your creation continues to amaze us as we explore the miracles of space, as we see into the very cells of our body. Yet we know that you placed all of these things in your world from the very beginning. Help us to accept change, we pray, but help us also to understand that some changes can be controlled and influenced by the way we live. Help us then, to change the things we can, to accept what we cannot change, and grant us wisdom so that we may know the difference. Amen.

Hymn
"Through all the changing scenes of life"

Program

In small groups, ask people to share some experiences of change in their lives. Begin with the most recent changes, then move on to exciting changes, important changes, amusing changes. After each discussion ask your group to note anything that remained constant during change. Was the constant element helpful?

Lead the discussion into changes that may have happened within your group, or within your faith community. Try to identify the changes as being well in the past, in the near past, or something that is happening at the present time. How long does the group feel it should take to adjust to some changes with your group or congregation? How long is too long? What should remain constant within a faith community as it undergoes change?

Is there a current opportunity to influence positive change? If there is, make plans to take action.

Is the old saying, "A change is as good as a rest" valid for your group?

CLOSING

Show the group the banner of the caterpillar and butterfly. Invite people to repeat the phrase "Change? Who me?" together, adding a "Yes" or "No" as they wish.

10

In Memorium

PREPARATION

It is traditional in some church groups to have an annual memorial service for members who have died during the year. If so, you may have particular customs, such as placing a flower on the worship center as each name is called. You would, therefore, need to make whatever arrangements may be required for that part of the service.

Another custom is to have members bring the names of those who have died to a meeting where this service is to be held. These can be read at the appropriate time, or the names may be written on slips of paper and collected and offered much the same as a monetary offering. Traditions vary; this service provides a base from which you may prepare a memorial service suitable to your group.

To use the closing section of the program you will need note paper and envelopes, pens and stamps, and a postal code directory, if possible.

Worship

Call to Worship

Jesus said, "I am the resurrection and the life..." Because of the life and resurrection of Jesus we are able to celebrate, rather than mourn, the deaths of friends and relatives. Come, then, let us worship and praise the God who is with us in life, in death, and beyond death.

Prayer

God of the living and the dead, God of the unborn and the new-born, we praise you for the cycle of life. We thank you that we live and move and have our being in your continual presence. We praise you for the faith that gives us a glimpse of a new way of being and for the sure and certain knowledge that we can never be separated from your love. As we remember those who have found that new way of being with you, we thank you for their lives among us, for their influence upon us, and for the ways in which they have expressed your love. Our prayers we offer in the name of the living Christ, Amen.

Hymn

"In the bulb there is a flower"

Scripture

1 Corinthians 13:1-13

(It could be suggested that people substitute in their minds the name of one or more of those being remembered whenever the word love is heard in the Scripture reading.)

Reflection

"For now we see in a mirror, dimly, but then we will see face to face. Now I know only in part; then I will know fully, even as I have been fully known." (1 Cor 13:12)

None of us knows everything about any of the people we are remembering today. Some were close friends, some mere acquaintances, others we had never met. It is not possible to know all there is to know about any other person, even members of our own families. Sometimes people do not wish us to know their inner thoughts. Sometimes we are so caught up with our own problems that we do not seek to really know those around us.

It is said there are four areas of knowledge in all of our lives. One part is known to ourselves and obvious to everyone else — things like the colour of our eyes, whether or not we wear glasses, our height and shape. A second part is made up of things about us that others know of which we are unaware — mannerisms, for instance, like the way our eyebrows rise when certain subjects come into conversation, or the way our eyes sparkle when we talk to children. The third part is a closely guarded part of ourselves, a part that we are reluctant to share. This might include details of personal relationships, deep fears, or anxieties. The fourth part is unknown even to ourselves: it is buried deep in what we call the subconscious. In getting to know another person, in getting to know ourselves, we need to explore the deeper parts of our lives. As we tell stories, laugh at one another's antics, we are enlarging the area that is known to ourselves and to others. This takes time, it takes effort, but it is the only way to change an acquaintance into a friend.

The people we are remembering today allowed others into their lives in very meaningful ways. They allowed themselves to be known by us. They shared a great deal of themselves through their involvement in our organization. As they worked with us, as they visited the sick and shut-ins, attended church suppers, and as they grieved with those who mourned and rejoiced with those who were celebrating, they became part of our lives, and we became part of theirs. And yet, each one of them held something back from us, something they are now able to disclose. Their fears are gone, their tears are wiped dry, their anxieties eased. They are known by God as they never dared to be known by us.

We also want to believe that they now understand why someone might have hurt them at some time. They are free to forgive, free to enjoy being completely open to whatever experiences their new existence provides. They did not take any grudges with them, and we can remember them without any guilt about what we might have done or said that we didn't do or say. It's all right! It's all right to remember them, to celebrate their lives, to recognize their influence upon us. To thank God for them. But do not grieve — rejoice! One day we too shall see clearly through the dark mirror we call death. One day we shall know and be fully known.

Ritual of Remembrance

Use one of the following rituals:

a / As names are read, flowers are placed in a vase at the worship center.

b / Slips of paper bearing the names of those to be remembered are collected and laid on the communion table or altar.

c / If there are not many names, someone could stand and say the name of the person and perhaps give a brief summary of their involvement in your group, or some outstanding characteristic.

d / Use your own familiar ritual, which may be different from A, B, or C, or some variation or combination.

Prayer

God of memory, we are thankful that you promised never to forget your people. May we continue to remember those who have served you, those whom we have known and loved, those who have left us to be with you. In our remembering we honour them. Our grief for them has been equal to the joy they gave us, and now we give you thanks for them. We pray that our remembering will help us to cherish the living of our lives and encourage us to be your faithful people all our days. In Jesus name we pray, Amen.

Hymn

"Now thank we all our God"

Program

Should a program be planned following the memorial service, begin by sharing stories of the people being remembered, asking group members to identify the characteristics or attitudes that made their lives memorable.

List the characteristics and attitudes on a flip chart.

How did our departed friends learn to be the kind of people they were? Where did these characteristics and attitudes come from?

How are people's values formed today? How do our children and our children's children learn to live the kind of lives that will invite people to honour their memory?

Closing

Provide note paper, envelopes, pens and stamps and ask all members of your group to write a note to the oldest person they know. Warn members not to include in the note the nature of the program that prompted it! Arrange to have these mailed.

Winter

11

"This Shall Be a Sign..."

PREPARATION

If your group members do not know one another well, make name tags from red octagons and yellow triangles, similar to STOP and YIELD road signs.

For the Program Section, write the four Scripture references — Deut 6:4-9, Ex 31:12-17, Ex 4:69, 1 Cor 1:22-25 — on small pieces of paper. Select four people to read these, and have them find the passage before the program begins.

You may wish to prepare some sort of sign for people to take home. A book mark is one possibility, or fridge magnets made of felt in the shape of small red hearts with a piece of magnetic tape on the back is another. You may know of something more appropriate to your own location or the particular time of year when the program is used. Be sure to tell people what the take-home item signifies.

WORSHIP

Call to Worship

"This shall be a sign for you: you will find a child wrapped in bands of cloth and lying in a manger." (Luke 2:12) That child grew to become our Saviour and Lord, and it is through him that we find the courage to approach our God in worship. Let us pray:

Prayer

Creator God, whose majesty surpasses anything we can imagine, we thank you for revealing yourself to us through your Son Jesus. In his name, and through the sign of his cross, we ask your blessing on our time together. Help us to understand that signs of your love and grace are all around us, if we but stop to look. Amen.

Hymn

"All beautiful the march of days"

Scripture

John 4:46-54

REFLECTION

There are three types of signs in the Bible. The first type of sign is a token, or symbol, of something important: God's rainbow sign, a token of God's promise to never destroy creation; Jacob's stones placed on the piece of ground where he wrestled with the angel as a sign of his experience; the monument the disciples wanted to put on the mountain top where they saw Jesus with Moses and Elijah would have identified another important place. Whether the sign is directly from God, or created by humans to symbolize a contact with God, it is a visible indication of invisible truths.

Signs can also indicate extraordinary happenings: signs seen as miracles. Some of these, such as Moses turning his stick into a serpent, or producing hordes of locusts, are a little hard to believe. Some people have problems with miraculous events recorded by the gospel writers as well. But they are signs of God's power. We believe that whatever happened at those particular times, God's presence and God's power were very real to the people involved.

The third type of sign in the Bible is referred to as heavenly. These are unusual events or happenings within the natural world. We are clearly told in Jeremiah that these particular signs are not always valid. "Do not be dismayed at the sign of the heavens," Jeremiah says, "for they are not to be trusted." He compares such signs to idolatry. In spite of this warning, the writers of the New Testament pointed out that it was a heavenly star that led the astrologers to the Christ child. Maybe one resolution to the conflict between those statements is contained in the word "led." The Magi did not assume to know all the answers from their observation of the star, they were simply willing to be guided by it.

In the first years following the death of Jesus, all of his followers believed they were living within a very measured amount of time. They looked for signs that Jesus would return before the end days. But Jesus himself tried to counteract this tendency, by criticizing the disciples' apparent need for some sort of sign, as we heard in the Scripture reading, and by telling them directly that no one would know when he would return — "But about that day and hour no one knows... for the Son of Man is coming at an unexpected hour."

Are there signs for us to see today, signs that can help us feel that God is still in control? If Jesus is not going to come again in our lifetime is God still with us? Lois Wilson, a former Moderator of the United Church of Canada, once said, "If you can see signs of hope, there *is* hope."

It is a hopeful sign to witness hundreds of people dedicating their lives in service to others, to notice caregivers providing loving care for the elderly and the disabled, to know that people

WINTER

willingly contribute time and money for medical research. The list goes on and on. We all know there is a down side to each of those signs of hope: those who serve others with only their own paycheque in mind, the depression that goes hand in hand with care giving, and the misuse or waste of money donated to research. But for the Christian the glass is always half full, never half empty. The Christian says, "Good Morning God," not "Good God, it's morning!" Because we *see* signs of hope, we believe there *is* hope, a hope that sustains us, energizes us, drives us. It joins us together in communities of faith and allows us to stand as a visible sign to our world, a sign that proclaims the mystery of our faith: Christ is dead, Christ is risen, Christ will come again.

Prayer

We confess, O God, that we often fail to see the signs of hope around us. Renew our inward sight, help us look beyond the commonplace, so that we recognize your spirit at work among us. We pray today for all who are looking for signs of comfort or healing, that they may be assured of your presence with them. We pray for those who mourn, who see signs of their loved ones all around them, that their memories may bring them only peace and joy. We pray for those who are lonely or depressed, that they may lift their eyes to see friendly, smiling faces; and we pray for ourselves, that we may be a visible witness of our faith to those we meet each day. In the name of Jesus, Amen.

PROGRAM

Begin by asking members of the group to share their favourite signs regarding the length and/or severity of winter, or their first signs of spring.

Have each of the four Scripture passages read, one at a time, following each reading with some discussion. You may use the suggested questions, or simply allow people to speak freely about what they understand from the reading.

Deuteronomy 6:4-9 (the instructions to the Jews to strengthen their memories of the Exodus) Signs as reminders, signs to tell people that we belong. How do we feel about people with religious pictures in their home? How can people tell that you're a Christian?

Exodus 31:12-17 (the significance of the Sabbath Day) Our regular worship is a sign of our faith. If our children do not see parents and grandparents in church, will they ever attend?

Exodus 4:69 (sign of power given to Moses by God) What are the signs of power in our world today? Do any of these signs come from God?

1 Corinthians 1:22-25 (Jews demand signs, but Christ is the power of God and the wisdom of God) Do we still think we need signs, or is Jesus Christ the only sign we need?

CLOSING

Close with the Mizpah Benediction, which for generations has been a sign of community and solidarity: "May the Lord watch between me and thee, while we are absent one from another." (Gen 31:49)

If you have prepared signs for members to take home, pass them out and share their significance.

12

Be Ye Flexible

PREPARATION

Purchase some colourful chenille pipe cleaners from a craft shop. Cut them so that you have half a pipe cleaner for each person expected. If you wish to extend the theme into your refreshments, how about some pretzels?

WORSHIP

Call to Worship

Blessed are the flexible, for they shall not be bent out of shape. Or should that be, Blessed are the flexible, for they can change shape when necessary? Our God was forced to be flexible, time and time again, as humans, loved by God, failed to hold their shape as the people of God. Then, God sent Jesus, to prove through the shape of a cross that our freedom to be flexible is always bound by love. Let us worship God.

Prayer

Our world has changed so much in our lifetime, O God, that we sometimes wonder if your rule of love will ever reach into the hardness of our hearts. We are grateful for the way our store of knowledge has increased; that you have helped us find ways to cure disease and fly to the moon. We rejoice that the inflexibility of stern rules and regulations that used to govern our societies has changed into a legal system that tries to uphold the rights of each individual. This has not always been easy, nor have we always lived up to what we know is right. Forgive us, we pray, and teach us how to love and care for one another. Amen.

Hymn

"Saviour, teach me day by day"

Scripture

John 14:21-27

REFLECTION

Saint Augustine is supposed to have said, "Love God and do as you please." Would that it were that simple. Bishop Robinson picked up on this concept in his book, *Honest to God*, written in the early 60's. It was the forerunner of what has been called situation ethics, meaning that instead of rules and regulations to define how we shall deal with specific problems in our society, we should instead be flexible enough to look at each situation, consider all the variables involved, and then act in love. This led to the humanization of the way we treat children born out of wedlock, for instance, or those whose marriage vows were broken. Some would say that it also led ultimately to the sexual revolution, the increase in teenage pregnancies and abortions and possibly even the AIDS epidemic.

Being flexible does not mean that we are prepared to lower our standards. Especially when the one standard by which we measure all else is love. Paul tells the Corinthians that love is not to be confined to some sloppy sort of sentimentalism. Love suffers, is kind, not envious or jealous or arrogant. It is not selfish, envious, or easily provoked. Love rejoices not in evil, but in truth; it "bears all things, believes all things, hopes all things, endures all things." There is room for flexibility in love, but never for unloving attitudes.

Inflexibility is most often found within faith communities when faced with change. Although the church has been changing continually throughout its history it never seems to do so without resistance. This can range from the often heard expression, "But we've *always* done it that way," when someone suggests some variety in the way communion is served, for example, or it can be as far reaching as inclusive language that asks us to reconsider the images we use to describe God and the words we use in worship and in our everyday speech. The fear that lies behind this resistance to change is rationalized in many different ways, but it is not often discussed in terms of a non-threatening, inclusive, love.

Consider the desire to change the way communion is served. Maybe it has been noted that attendance is low on communion Sundays because of the length of the service. What is the loving way to react to this situation? By saying that people *should* be willing to stay as long as it takes, or attempting to modify the service so that it retains its meaningfulness but takes less time?

Our language is becoming more inclusive. Nothing will change that. What, then, is the loving response to people who wish to use some feminine images of God? Should we refuse, on the grounds that the Bible refers to God as He, or should we be open to discovering the feminine images of God found in the Scriptures but ignored for centuries? Do we alienate some people to hold on to others, or can we recognize the validity of different viewpoints and try to build bridges from one to the other? To do so will require a very flexible faith community, one that is open, inclusive and willing to follow the leading of the Holy Spirit.

Prayer

Gracious God, we hope that you understand us when we say that we no longer wish to be broken, melted, and molded into a particular kind of vessel for you to use. Help us, we pray, to be willing to take whatever shape life demands of us, to be flexible enough to adapt to new and challenging avenues of service. We need to know that your love will never change, but we ask your guidance as we seek to put that love into the type of action that tries to meet the needs of our world today. Amen.

PROGRAM

Young people might enjoy one of those games (i.e. "Twister") where you put hands and feet in designated spots on a game sheet and end up in quite a tangle! Or have members stand in a circle with hands outstretched to the center of the circle. Grasp someone else's hands and then try to face the *outside* of the circle without breaking the contacts. This will hopefully indicate flexibility without the risk of serious injury.

Ask members to individually indicate one situation, something that is relative to today's world, where they would never be willing to make a compromise. Is there an area in life, besides the obvious ones of murder, drug pushing, arson, etc., where they would have to say, as Luther did, "Here I stand, before God I can do no other"?

Ask if anyone has participated in a demonstration that involved civil disobedience, such as refusing to obey certain laws because of a moral conviction and indicating this through passive resistance. If so, ask that person to share their feelings and explain how they made the decision to become involved. If not, ask if there is anything that people would consider worthy of civil disobedience. Is there any flexibility involved in such actions? What would a loving, flexible solution look like?

What would be a loving thing for your group to do within your faith community that would indicate your willingness to be flexible? Make it so.

CLOSING

Give each person present one half of a pipe cleaner. Pipe cleaners are very flexible, and can be bent into or out of shape very easily! Ask people to make a heart shape from their pipe cleaner, but note that even love changes its shape under pressure. Suggest that they be put somewhere where they can remind people of the need to be flexible while retaining their integrity as loving children of God.

13

Money Matters

PREPARATION

This program would provide a useful kick-off for an interesting fund-raiser. Called "talent money," the idea is to give each member of a group two dollars. They are to take the money and use their talents to increase it. This can be done through home baking, craft items, or the profits from babysitting or tutoring — anything that indicates how they have used their God-given talents. Some may simply return the money after the designated amount of time has elapsed, others may wish to simply add to the original amount.

If you decide to use this idea, you would need to have the money available to give group members at the end of the meeting. To make sure that everyone understands the project, distribute the money with a photocopy of the poem *Talent Money*, found in the resource section.

WORSHIP

All that I have, all that I am. Saying "Yes" to Jesus means that everything we own or possess or enjoy is ours only in trust; his call has always been a call to total commitment. Sell all you have; follow me. Acknowledging our human desire to look after ourselves first, let us begin our worship with a prayer of confession. Let us pray:

Prayer
Loving God, we have taken your love for granted, often forgetting that we have a responsibility to love others, to care for others, as your Son taught. Our selfish natures help us to survive in the physical world, but our spiritual natures are unsatisfied unless we learn to share. Forgive our unwillingness to risk sharing more of the gifts we have received through your grace, and teach us that it *is* more blessed to give than to receive. In Jesus' name we pray. Amen.

Assurance of Pardon
We may recognize that there is some selfishness or greed within us but confessing this before God and before one another assures us of God's immediate forgiveness. Forgiven, we may need to try a little harder, but we do so confident that God is with us all the way.

Hymn
"Take my life and let it be"

Scripture
Matthew 19:16-26

REFLECTION

It is difficult to find something new to say about stewardship. It is something we all believe in, something we have heard about many times in programs and sermons. It could be said that Stewardship is something that is given *lip service* by church people, like singing hymns without giving conscious thought to the words.

There is one aspect of stewardship that seems to be omitted, even from the honest attempts to be good stewards of our treasures, our time, our talents, our tissue and our terrain. What we often omit is an emphasis on the *sacramental* nature of giving. There may not be a formal liturgy for receiving the offering, as there is for baptism or communion, but have you ever noticed that in most churches the congregation never needs to be prompted to stand as the offering is received? It seems to be a very familiar action, familiar because we *always* stand to present our offering! During worship we stand to sing and sit to listen, usually. We also stand to give respect, as when mourners enter the church during a funeral, and it may be our respect for the place of money in the life of our faith community that brings us to our feet.

Probably the best illustration of the sacramental nature of giving found in the Bible is in the gospel of John, Chapter 12:1-8, where Mary poured expensive ointment over the head of Jesus. Some were shocked, but Jesus understood that this was something holy, something sacred, something *sacra*mental. When we can learn to give with such abandon, such recklessness, such love, then we will feel as good about our giving as we do when we share the Eucharist, or watch an infant being baptized.

Prayer

All that we are, all that we have, comes from you, O God. Help us to offer it back in response. Help us to see our money as something holy, our whole life as a sacred trust. Let us learn to make our giving a sacrament offered in love. We ask this in the name of the One who gave everything, your Son, Jesus. Amen.

Program

Ask group members to do a little mental arithmetic. They do not need to share the results.

1. Estimate the cost of the clothes and jewelry you are wearing right now.

2. What was the cost of the last item you purchased for any reason?
3. Approximately how much money do you have in your possession right now?
   Add 1, 2 and 3 before you go on to the next question.
4. How much did you put in your church envelope last Sunday?
5. How much will you put in next Sunday?

For most of us there is a great difference between what we spend on ourselves and what we contribute to the church. Few people tithe, giving the church ten percent of their income, as the Bible recommends. It has been suggested that if each family with an earned income were to give only two percent to their church there would be no need of holding teas, suppers, or bazaars in order to raise money to meet the budget.

Discuss the pros and cons of fund-raising within a faith community.

The reflection suggests there is a sacramental nature to the money we give as offering. Do members of the group agree? Discuss how people feel about the idea.

How can we reconcile the desire to decorate our sanctuaries with stained glass or to purchase new choir gowns or a new organ with the sacramental nature of money?

Where do our outreach ministries fit into the picture? Is it easier to ask people to bring donations for a food bank than to support community projects through a church budget? Why?

CLOSING

If you take an offering at your meetings, have it received before the program begins. Place it in a prominent place before the group and stand to dedicate the offering at the close of the meeting. If there is no traditional offertory prayer in your group, you could use the following:

Prayer

Eternal God, whose extravagant love towards us is best shown in the gift of your Son Jesus, accept these offerings as tokens of our response to that gift, as indications of our love for our church, the body of Christ. Make us cheerful givers, O God, not only of our possessions, but of ourselves. Amen.

14

Living Today

PREPARATION

Pin up extra calendars, with the date of your meeting circled in red. Enlarge the date and make some photocopies of it to pin up as well. Have copies of the current daily newspaper available. You may think of other ways to focus members attention on today. A flip chart would be useful for the program section.

WORSHIP

Call to Worship

This is the day that the Lord has made; let us rejoice and be glad in it! Now is the acceptable time of the Lord, and it is now that we lift our hearts and minds in praise and thanksgiving to the God who is here with us at this very moment. Let us sing what has just been said:

Hymn
"This is the day, this is the day"

Scripture
Matthew 6:25-34

Reflection

Hundreds of books and articles have been written on the importance of cherishing the present time. We have been warned that we should not live in the past, or the future, but in the here and now. Yesterday is dead, it is said, forget it; tomorrow is not here, don't worry; today is here — use it! We all know of the successful slogan of the AA movement, where those addicted to alcohol seek to abstain "just for today." Another poster says that "those who miss the journey may miss about all they're going to get," indicating that we should seek to enjoy life as we live it, rather than thinking of it as going somewhere, or achieving something.

Wise words, maybe, but much easier to say than to live by. We cannot escape our past, and most of us wouldn't want to anyway. We cherish memories of our childhood, and our children's childhoods. We remember good times with friends now living in distant places. Sometimes we wish that we had made different decisions in our past, or made more effort to attain a goal now far beyond our reach, but we know that we must accept the past because we cannot change it.

And many of us fear the future. We're not sure that we will have enough money to look after ourselves if we, or our partner, should become unable to work. We look at the state of the world and we wonder what opportunities will be available for the young people in our midst. We read about the ozone layer and we put on sun block and hope our future doesn't include skin cancer. We envy those who can eat, drink and be merry, yet consider them irresponsible. If everyone lived completely in the present, who would plan for future generations?

None of this prevents us from living this very moment as though eternity was around the corner, or as if it was the very last day of our lives. All of our complaints are relative: a paper cut can be painful to a healthy person, while someone with chronic arthritis regards getting out of bed in the morning without severe pain as a blessing. Headaches and colds make us all feel miserable but knowing someone with Multiple Sclerosis or terminal cancer can make complaining about such things seem very selfish. Again, all physical pain or discomfort is relative to our usual state of health. We need to learn to say with St. Paul, "for I have learned, in whatsoever state I am, therewith to be content." (Philippians 4:11b, King James Version)

Let us then remember all the advice we have heard from our parents, from bumper stickers, from the Bible, and from self-help books, and resolve to choose one that helps us live today with a positive attitude. Write it on your hearts, remind yourself of it throughout the day, and thank God every evening if you were able to "have a nice day!"

PROGRAM

Begin by soliciting from members the various slogans and Bible verses that encourage us to live life one day at a time. Write these on a flip chart.

These points for positive living have evolved because so many people find it difficult to leave the past behind, or to stop fretting about the future. Why do you think so many people have trouble enjoying the here and now?

Ask members of the group to close their eyes and visualize their pasts. Allowing a minute or two between questions, guide them by asking: Where is your past situated in your imagination — in front of you, behind you, over or above, or left or right? What colours are in your past? What event stands out most clearly?

Picture a container of some sort that will hold your past. Try to fit everything into it. Store it somewhere, in a place where you will be able to find it easily, but where it will be safe. A shelf, a closet, the trunk of your car, in your first home maybe. When your past is safely tucked away, open your eyes.

If people wish to share some of the places where they have placed their pasts, they may, but it is not essential. Move on and do the same thing with the future: Where is it? What colours are there? What would be in your future if you could place anything you wanted there? Is there something here that disturbs you? Name it in your mind and give it a definite shape. It may be illness in the shape of a white hospital bed, or death in the form of flowers at a funeral. We cannot store these as we did with things in our past. We must instead insist that they stay in our future, not in our present. To do this we could place them in outer space, hang them on a star, or give them to a giant squid who lives in the deepest part of the sea. When the future is out of your way, open your eyes.

Now ask people to look around them, to notice the people in the room, the furniture in the room, the temperature, the comfort or discomfort of the chairs and anything else that is reality at this particular moment in time. Enjoy all of it!

CLOSING

Campers in your group may remember the lines of a poem called, "Salutation to the Dawn," which dates back to the Sanskrit, circa 1200 BCE. It would be an appropriate closing:

Look to this day!
For it is Life, the very Life of Life.
In its brief course lie all the
Verities and Realities of your Existence:
  The Bliss of Growth,
  The Glory of Action,
  The Splendor of Beauty,
For Yesterday is but a Dream,
And To-morrow is only a Vision:
But To-day well-lived makes
Every Yesterday a Dream of Happiness,
And every To-morrow a Vision of Hope.
Look well therefore to this Day!

Spring

15

Rooted and Built Up

WORSHIP

Call to Worship

God must have the greatest green thumb ever known — all the plants of the planet owe their creation and their survival to our God. As we enjoy the bounty of the earth, let us resolve to be good caretakers and to honour the Creator. Let us worship the God of all earth's gardens.

Prayer

God of the garden of Eden and of our backyards, we often feel your presence while we are planting, pruning, or enjoying our gardens. We can believe in eternal life when we plant dry bulbs and see them mature into daffodils and tulips. We believe in your covenant love when a rainbow arches over the trees. In the balance of nature we recognize your care for the world you have created, and we pray for the wisdom to be good gardeners of your earth. Amen.

Hymn

"All beautiful the march of days" or "All things bright and beautiful"

Scripture

Colossians 2:6-15

REFLECTION

In the reading from Colossians we heard the words of the apostle Paul, "As you therefore have received Christ Jesus the Lord, continue to live your lives in him, rooted and built up in him and established in the faith, just as you were taught, abounding in thanksgiving."

Summertime is the ideal time to talk about "being rooted and built up." No longer springtime, when we set out the seedlings and admire the beautiful fresh green of leaves and plants. Not yet harvest, when we can celebrate the results of the year's growth, and find ourselves pickling, canning, freezing, and trying to get rid of the zucchinis. Summer is the time when those plants that are going to produce the harvest must be firmly rooted, and built up. Corn, for instance, needs to have the soil piled up at the base of the plant, or the whole plant will topple over in the slightest wind. Plants must be strong to resist the hot sun, insects, too much rain or too little rain. This is where all our weeding and fertilizing and hoeing brings results. If we have been good gardeners, if all our plants have taken hold, we can expect an abundant harvest.

Paul's letter to the Colossians was a bit like a T.V. gardening show. It was an offer of help. The Colossians were having problems. The faith that they had been so excited about just didn't seem to be taking root. Paul's letter to them addressed these problems.

The town of Colossae was in Asia Minor, east of Ephesus. Paul felt responsible for this area, although it was Epaphras, one of Paul's workers, who had gone to Colossae from Ephesus and who had first brought the Christian faith to the town. We don't know what happened, but it seems as though there were some traditional leaders, Jewish Christians, in that new faith community who wanted to make some strict rules. They were insisting on the Hebrew law of circumcision, for instance. Circumcision is a naming rite of the Jewish faith, somewhat similar to our infant baptism. Many of the early Christians, including Jesus, were circumcised Jews. Gentiles who embraced the faith, however, were not required to be circumcised. There were other rules and regulations, about which foods could be eaten, and which could not, and there were special holy days to be observed and so on. As in most congregational struggles, it was probably a question of power; having people obey rules that you establish gives you a feeling of power over them. Something had happened between the sowing of the seed by Epaphras and the anticipated generous harvest of a vital, energizing community of faith.

Paul heard about the struggles of this faith community, and he sent this letter to Colossae by a worker named Tychicus. In the letter Paul points out that only Jesus is Saviour and Lord, and that these other leaders are actually leading people away from the true faith. Since you have accepted Christ, he says, keep your roots deep in him, build your lives on him. Forget the rules and regulations of church people who put themselves in leadership positions, there is only one person with absolute authority regarding our faith and that is Jesus, the Christ, author and finisher of the faith. For a community of faith to develop properly, it, like the plants in a garden, needed careful nurturing and lots of tender, loving care. It needed to be firmly rooted in Jesus and built up by continually meeting together to study, learn, pray and to share together in the breaking of bread.

Prayer

Loving God, as we cultivate our gardens or as we admire gardens others have maintained, we thank you for the roots of faith that support our community. We thank you for all who have gone before us, whose dedication and perseverance has made our work easier. Help us to pass on our skills, so that the future church will grow and flourish, rooted and built up in communion with your Son, Jesus, in whose name we pray. Amen.

PROGRAM

Introduce this Bible study by asking members to share their ideas about the words in the passage, rooted and built up. Most people will recognize that deep roots hold plants firmly in place, protecting them from wind and rain and providing a way for them to receive food from the ground. Being built up could refer to some heavy plants, like corn, which need additional soil at their roots. The gardener must pull the soil up around the plant to give it support. Sometimes roots are not enough!

Move on to what it means to be rooted and built up in Jesus Christ.

Can we relate building up to the need to provide support for marginalized people in our society? Is affirmative action a type of "building up?"

In the letter to the Colossians there is an indication that it is the leaders of the faith community in Colossae who are causing the conflict. Can this be related to the leadership of our own faith community? In our country? How can we be sure that our leaders are taking us in the right direction?

There are two expressions that may provoke some discussion:

- If a leader gets too far ahead of the followers, the leader is not leading, he or she is just taking a walk!
- If leaders get too far ahead of the followers, they find themselves alone.

Paul suggests that Jesus is our ultimate authority, not our leaders. How can we reconcile respect for those in leadership positions with our commitment to be followers of Jesus Christ?

CLOSING

Each year our gardens assure us that seed time and harvest will continue. The miracle of the Christian Church is that, in spite of some poor leadership and indifferent followers, the Church has survived, and will survive. Let these (seeds, bulbs) assure all of us that indeed, life goes on. Thanks be to God.

SPRING

16

Woman's Place

PREPARATION

From your personal experience list on a flip chart the occupation or life interest of women in families you know, including as many generations as possible. For instance, a great-grandmother, grandmother or mother may have been a housewife, partner with a husband farming or fishing, or someone who never married in order to care for parents. Someone in the next generation may have worked part-time, or taught or nursed. What about the current generation? Are there any women in non-traditional careers? Does your list indicate that women have "come a long way?"

WORSHIP

Call to Worship

When Mary found her place at the foot of the cross where her beloved friend Jesus was slowly dying, she made a claim for the right of all women to share in Christ's ministry. The woman who reached out to touch the hem of Jesus' garment was daring to say, "I have a right to a place beside this man." And so, centuries later, women throughout the world are reclaiming their place, their right to be wherever their dreams take them. Women's place, the place of people everywhere, is near to the heart of God. Let us find our way to that place through our worship.

Prayer

We approach you with confidence, O God, recognizing that you know all of us by name, you would gather us under your wing as a hen gathers her chicks. We are held in the palm of your hand, and we thank you for the awareness of your presence that these images invoke. Support us in our struggles when we or someone close to us must claim a new place in family or society; strengthen us when others would put us "in our place." Do not, we pray, let us stray from your loving care. Amen.

Hymn

"Near to the heart of God" or "Beneath the cross of Jesus"

REFLECTION

A popular slogan of the 90's says that a woman's place is in the House — and the Senate. We have come through a cultural revolution during which many women have worked hard to achieve gender equality. We have also experienced a backlash to that revolution, made evident in increased violence against women and resentment toward any form of affirmative action. But a song cannot be unsung, nor can words be unsaid. There is no turning back.

As we begin to read the Bible with minds more open to the stories of women, we find countless examples of women who refused to be stereotyped. Women like the Hebrew midwives, who disobeyed the law of the land by allowing Hebrew babies to survive. The woman who insisted that she and her family deserved more than crumbs like those thrown under the table for dogs. There is Mary, who wanted to talk with Jesus while her sister acted as hostess, and Lydia, whose income and social position enabled her to have part of the early church meet in her home.

Although the stories of these women were recorded in the Bible, they were seldom used as role models for women in any patriarchal society. Listen to this story of a 20th century woman who knew her Bible well, but who still firmly believed that her place was to be a helpmate for her husband, a homemaker and caregiver. She also felt that her *place* was on a lower social level than many other people, and she was content to have it so.

Minnie was born at the turn of the century and lived in a small village where her widowed mother struggled to support three children. She began working as a housemaid at age fourteen, and for the next fourteen years she moved from house to house, until she met and married a man apprenticed to a plumber. They had a good marriage, two children, and a continually-increasing standard of living. The woman, however, always seemed to know that her place was in the home, caring for her children, cooking and cleaning for her family. She was never able to feel equal to women like those for whom she had worked. When her husband became a well-respected businessman she still had one tone of voice when speaking to family members on the telephone, and another for customers. This may seem like an insignificant comment, but to her children it emphasized the class structure of their world. Their mother was a nice, quiet person; she was patient and loving, but reserved.

Minnie dreamed of being a missionary, but realized that such a lofty calling was completely out of her reach. She was instead a faithful member of the Women's Missionary Society, and sang the missionary hymns with quiet zeal. The family attended church faithfully, and she was pleased when her adult children began to participate in the life of the congregation. She was thrilled when her daughter married a minister, though she was adamant that she expected her grandchildren to take precedence over work, volunteer or otherwise, on the part of her daughter. Unfortunately, she died before her granddaughter was ordained, without knowing how much impact her acceptance of her place in life would encourage daughter and granddaughter to seek a different one.

This is not an uncommon story. Many women of former generations accepted their roles as wife, mother and housekeeper without question. They also accepted the fact of class distinction. There were rich people; there were poor people. There was always someone a little worse off than yourself, but there was little envy of those who were much better off, either financially or educationally. "Just as I am" might well have meant "and as I always shall be."

There is much merit in accepting one's lot in life. There is no point in putting ourselves down because we live in a developed country and have a good job while there are people sleeping in the streets in less developed countries, and often in our own. Maybe it is impossible for *everyone* to live the good life, but our challenge is to live in tension between ourselves and the world around us as it is right now, and our dream of what we and our world could become. Our mission is to work towards the dream of complete equality, a world where each person is seen and known and loved as a child of God and where people have an equal chance to reach their own potential.

Prayer

Complete equality may never be possible, dear God, because it would entail an end to war and disease, a complete restructuring of world society. Nevertheless we believe that working towards that equality is a way to identify with your will and purpose for your creation. Help us to believe that each person who achieves their full potential is a step towards your will being done, on earth as it is in heaven. Help us to be part of making it so. Amen.

PROGRAM

Refer to your list of women and their various occupations or interests. (See Preparation.) Discuss the changes that have taken place during the past twenty or thirty years. Identify women who were able to overcome the "women's place is in the home" syndrome — can you find reasons why they were able to break the mold? (Things like well-educated parents, wealth, or very strong personality.) Identify also women who have worked outside the home and found the experience lacking in something important to them. Is this also breaking a mold, a modern one? Allow enough time for as many stories as possible.

A radical feminist once said, "If it weren't for us radicals, you moderates wouldn't get anywhere." Discuss this statement. Is it true that humans seem to go from one extreme to the other in many areas? (Examples: bottle/breast feeding, short/long skirts, parental permissiveness/parental discipline, etc.)

Share ideas of how members can help young people achieve their full potential. Try to come up with some specific method of affirming the young people in your faith community, with some special attention (affirmative action) placed on young girls. For example, hold a special career day for pre-teen girls.

CLOSING

Stand in a circle, to indicate that all those present have a place in your group. Ask everyone to take a step towards the center of the circle, which should bring everyone close enough for a group hug.

17

Blessings

PREPARATION

Prepare some blessings: messages of cheer or courage printed on small slips of paper. If you are really ambitious, you could buy fortune cookies and replace their fortunes with your blessings. Or, simply roll the pieces of paper and secure with a tiny piece of ribbon or tape.

WORSHIP

Call to Worship

In the Hebrew Scriptures the first recorded blessing is the one given to Abraham when he was challenged to move to a strange new land. In the New Testament, the angel tells Mary that she is blessed among women. As Christians we consider ourselves blessed by the gift of God's son, Jesus. Let us praise and worship the God who saw all of creation as good, the God whose blessing we continue to both seek and acknowledge.

Prayer

Creator God, origin of all blessing, we thank you for your care and your love. We thank you for your presence among us, for your Spirit working within us. Grant, we pray, that we may be worthy of all that you offer us so freely, and that we may show forth your love and praise, not only with our lips, but through lives of loving service. Amen.

Scripture

Genesis 12:1-4, 13:14-18

Hymn

"Bless and keep us, God" or "Blest be the tie that binds"

REFLECTION

The words blessing, blessed, blesses, or bless, are found over four hundred times in the New Revised Standard version of the Bible. It was a very significant concept for the writers of both Old and New Testaments. The dictionary definition of the word offers such things as "to give thanks to; to consecrate; to invoke happiness on; or to make happy." We use the word in these ways as we pray, saying, "We bless you God (meaning we give thanks) for all your kindness towards us." Or, "Bless (as in consecrate) the gifts we offer" and "Bless (or make happy, keep safe) our friends and family." There is a chorus sung in some faith communities that says, "Make me a blessing." This connects with the idea of God being within each and every one of us, so that we are all capable of giving thanks, consecrating gifts, especially our own talents or abilities, or making other people happy.

Apart from worship services, the blessing we hear most often these days is probably the "Bless you" or "God bless you" we casually say to someone who has just sneezed. It was felt in years gone by that the Spirit (breath) was leaving the body when a person sneezed, and the blessing was offered as a protection. It was as though God's presence needed to be restored in some way. Modern science indicates that sneezing is indeed a rather major happening within the human body; some have said that we are closest to death when we sneeze. Blessing someone in such a precarious situation may not be such a bad idea.

"Bless you" is also another way of saying, "I love you." In one family the teenage children became tired of hearing their mother say, "Be careful" every time they left in the car. They felt that their mother didn't trust them. When she explained that "be careful" was just another way of saying "I love you" they began responding to her parting words with a cheerful, "We love you too, Mom!" The sad part of that story is the difficulty so many of us have in actually saying those particular phrases, both "I love you" and "God bless you."

The sacrament of baptism and the marriage ceremony invoke blessing on the new baby or the new relationship. Centered in community, they indicate that love and support will be provided to make the blessing visible and practical. Times of blessing are happy times — birthdays, anniversaries, retirements, or any occasion where we take a little effort to express the love we feel for friends and family. We often express this love through greeting cards, flowers, parties or gifts; an indirect way of asking God to bless the recipients.

Although the language is neither inclusive nor contemporary, for many people there is a familiarity about the benediction found in the sixth chapter of the book of Numbers that makes it a very meaningful blessing:

"The Lord bless you, and keep you. The Lord make his face to shine upon you, and be gracious unto you. The Lord lift up his countenance upon you, and give you peace."

Program

Spend some fun time counting your blessings, asking each person to think of something that isn't normally on our list of things for which we are thankful. (Some suggestions: watches and alarm clocks, stuffed toys, the smell of a new baby, chocolate, and maybe someone will suggest plumbing, or microwaves.) Continue by naming people or institutions that you would like God to bless.

The blessing upon which both the Jewish and Christian faiths are based is the one found in the book of Genesis, Chapter 12:

Now the Lord said to Abraham, "Go from your county and your kindred and your father's house to the land that I will show you. I will make of you a great nation, *and I will bless you*, and make your name great, so that you will be a blessing."

Discuss the significance of this blessing, and the covenant that follows, (See Genesis 17:1-8) both for Jews and Christians.

How have Christians attempted to be a blessing to the world? Have we always been successful? Lead into a discussion around the change in the church's sense of mission: rather than taking western culture along with the gospel to people in developing countries, today's Christians are more involved in encouraging development in such places by working in partnership with indigenous people. Can providing equipment to dig wells be as much of a blessing as telling people about Jesus? Do we need to do both? How can we recognize the spirituality of people who have never heard of Jesus? What about people in our own country who are oblivious to any form of spirituality, who have no Christian memory, how can we be a blessing to them? Can you give some examples?

Close by asking people to think of ways in which they could try being a blessing during the coming week.

Closing

Distribute the blessings you have prepared. If there is time, and if numbers permit, have people read them aloud. In larger groups they could be shared with one or two people in the group and then taken home to remind them that counting our blessings should be a daily habit.

18

Visiting

PREPARATION

Very little preparation is necessary for this program. Presumably the leader will have some idea of the amount of visiting presently being done by the group and whether the emphasis should be on supporting a current visitation program or encouraging more visiting. This information will influence the discussion in the Program section, if used.

WORSHIP

Call to Worship

One of the earliest stories in the New Testament tells of the visit of Mary to her cousin, Elizabeth. There Mary received support and encouragement; there her "yes" to God's call was confirmed and validated. We cannot support one another in isolation, and we cannot receive God's grace if we do not learn to recognize the gift through our worship. Let us pray:

Prayer

Gracious God, you have visited your people throughout history in ways that are often beyond our imagination: in a burning bush, a ladder to heaven, a loaf of bread, a cup of wine. But you have also been present in the visit of a friend, a neighbour or a church member, people who visit in the name of the church, in the name of your Son. Having received, help us to give. Give us confidence, we pray, that we may reach out to the people around us in meaningful ways. Amen.

Hymn

"Jesus, united by your grace"

Scripture

Matthew 25:31-46

REFLECTION

Some women's church groups are very proud of the amount of visiting they do. At each meeting the number of visits is recorded along with roll call. Years ago these numbers were reported to regional and national counterparts, and it was recognized that community friendship and visiting was a vital part of the program of the group.

Whether or not these numbers are still recorded, and regardless of their increase or decrease, many church groups are actively involved in a visiting program. Part of our identity as members of a particular faith community involves, among other things, visiting the sick, the lonely, the bereaved, and newcomers in our midst.

What happens during one of these visits varies with the visitor and those being visited. Sometimes conversation centers around the weather, or health problems. In stewardship visitations, money and the financial situation of our church becomes the topic. If our presence in the home of another person is the only requirement to qualify it as a visit, we may be missing an opportunity to share our faith or to discover the unmet needs of the person we are visiting. When Jesus visited the home of Mary and Martha, his physical needs were well looked after by Martha, but he, in turn, was able to meet Mary's need to be more actively involved in his ministry. How we wish we had a record of that discussion between Mary and Jesus! It would have been an excellent model for us to use in our visiting. Did he inquire about her health? Or did he talk about himself? Did he ask questions that helped Mary share any problems she might have been having? Were they talking about practical things, like the next place Jesus planned to visit, or were they talking about the way Jesus was able to change people's idea of God?

There are certain skills that are invaluable when it comes to visiting. We need to know when to draw people out, when to sense their unwillingness to share. We need ears that hear unspoken words, eyes to see beyond physical appearances, and hearts that are open to another's sorrow or joy. Many of these skills can be learned, many are skills that we already possess but neglect to use intentionally when we visit. Maybe the most important skills for use in visiting are a simple smile and a warm hug.

Prayer

Loving God, whose smile is all creation, help us bring cheer and love to those we visit. Help us to share the joy we experience as followers of your Son, Jesus. We believe he enjoyed visiting friends, and we know that many people sought out his companionship. We thank you for making us social creatures, O God, people who need people. In our visiting help us to see you in the people we meet, to minister to them, and in so doing to be open to their ministry to us. In Jesus name we pray, Amen.

PROGRAM

There are many videos that help to "train" visitors for church visitations. Investigate your own denomination's resources. There are also people in most communities who would be willing to speak to your group about visiting skills — social workers, ministers, chaplains, health care workers. If you would like to facilitate talk about such skills in your group without calling in an expert, the following guidelines may be useful:

Role play (act out) one or two typical visiting situations. Take only a few minutes for each one, and allow time following each role play for people to move out of the role they were assuming and back into their own character. This may be done with a few simple questions, such as, "How did it feel to be a visitor in that situation?" or "Would you have responded to the caller differently if you were being visited yourself?"

1st Situation

Mary is visiting the Jones family. It is a regular friendship visit and Mary doesn't know that Mr. Jones has recently lost his job and the youngest child needs new sneakers to play in a basketball tournament.

2nd Situation

Joe is doing a financial campaign visit to the Smith family. He knows that the Smith's haven't been in church much lately, but doesn't know why. The Smith's are staying away because someone threw out the cookies Mrs. Smith sent to the bake sale, saying they were burnt.

3rd Situation

Sarah, a member of a seniors group, is visiting the Brown family to encourage them to participate in their activities. Mrs. Brown dominates the conversation by complaining about the long sermons preached by the new minister.

Follow each role play with discussion on the way each visitor handled the situation. Do not be judgemental, and assume that any bad visiting habits were done to illustrate what *not* to do. If possible, develop some guidelines for visiting within your own group.

Lent

19

Lenten Table Conversation

PREPARATION

Plan a pot luck supper for your group. Try to arrange the seating so that people are facing one another. The arrangement will vary, of course, with the size of your group: a square where all sit on the outside, a T-shaped arrangement or smaller tables seating four or six.

Water glasses, rolls, salt shakers and mustard seeds are needed as props for the table conversation. Recruit volunteer helpers and photocopy the program for those taking part.

ASKING THE BLESSING

Before people begin to gather their food, have them join hands while someone asks the blessing. If there is a member who is renowned for meaningful table blessings, by all means ask him or her to do so. Or the following could be used:

Be present at these tables, Lord, as you were present with the disciples as they shared that memorable meal in the Upper Room. As we eat may we find nourishment for our bodies. As we talk and listen may we find the spiritual food we crave. Be present as our unseen guest, we pray, as you are present with us throughout all of our living and loving. Amen.

CONVERSATION FOLLOWING THE MEAL

Leader: *The food we have eaten is very different from the food that the disciples ate in the Upper Room. That was a Passover Meal, a solemn ceremony re-enacted every year by Jewish families. In some ways the Pot Luck Supper has become a ritual for faith communities in North America. It is our way of sharing food and being together as people who have much in common.*

1st helper: But we don't usually have any ceremony or ritual with our pot luck supper, and if we do, we wait until we've cleared away the dishes.

2nd helper: And often we move into the church sanctuary for worship.

3rd helper: I don't know if I can really feel like I'm worshipping when all these dirty dishes are left on the table.

Leader: *But there are things on these tables* **(this table)** *that could provide a real spiritual blessing for us, if we look for the meaning behind them.*

2nd helper: I suppose you mean things like the salt? Jesus said that we are the salt of the earth.

Leader:	*That's right. And if salt loses its flavor it has to be thrown out.*
1st helper:	Salt sort of wakes up your taste buds. I read a book once, called *Salty Christians*. To be salty is to be alive, to be active.
Leader:	*Let's all taste the salt to remind us to be salty people — active and really alive!*

(Each person shakes a little salt into the palm of their hand and tastes it with their tongue.)

3rd helper:	A certain minister always worried about what would happen if everyone brought pickles to a pot luck supper. There are some pickles here, and they have mustard seeds in them. I see that someone has provided little dishes of mustard seeds as well — is that to remind us that even a tiny bit of faith can move mountains?
Leader:	*Yes, that is a very familiar illustration for most of us. It comes from the gospel of Matthew, where Jesus tells his disciples , "... if you have faith the size of a mustard seed, you will say to this mountain, 'Move from here to there,' and it will move; and nothing will be impossible for you." (Matthew 17:20) Now let's each try to pick one seed out of the dish to remind us how very small these mustard seeds are.*

(Pass the dishes of mustards seeds and have everyone try to take out just one.)

1st helper:	There are many seeds that are smaller than these, I wonder why Jesus chose the mustard seed?

2nd helper: Probably because where Jesus lived the mustard seed produces quite a large tree, not just the mustard plant that we know. It's all relative, you know.

3rd helper: Mighty oaks from tiny acorns, for instance.

Leader: *But it's faith that Jesus was talking about, not trees! We don't need to be theological scholars or to spend hours in prayer to have faith. And if we have even a little bit of faith it can move mountains of doubt, of despair, or it can help us do great things for God.*

3rd helper: So that's salt and mustard. What else do we have here?

2nd helper: We have water. Water is a powerful symbol. It is life itself, for nothing can live without it. Water cleanses too, and it constantly renews itself. Jesus washed the disciples' feet with water, and water mixed with blood came from the sword wound in his side at his crucifixion. In baptism, water symbolizes commitment to Christ and his teachings.

Leader: *Since we have finished our meal, it is safe for us to put our fingers into our water glasses, and then to touch those wet fingers to the forehead of our neighbour around the table. This will remind us of our own baptism.*

(Beginning with the leader, or one designated person at each table, fingers are dipped in water and then placed on the forehead of the next person. The words "(First name) you are a child of God." may be said as this is done.)

1st helper: What about this roll? It can remind us that Jesus told us that we should be like yeast.

Leader: *That's right. The yeast has made the roll light and good to eat, but you can't taste the yeast, can you? The church in the world needs to be active like yeast, without drawing attention to itself through pomp and ceremony. And it's the same for individual Christians, who can serve without expecting rewards.*

2nd helper: The roll can certainly remind us of the Last Supper. Jesus said that it could represent his body. "Take, eat," were his words that night, "This is my body."

Leader: *Yes, to continue the Passover tradition, where unleavened bread is used to symbolize the hurried way the Hebrews fled from the Egyptians, Jesus said his followers could remember him through the eating of bread. He broke the bread, to indicate the coming broken-ness of his own body.*

3rd helper: Jesus said that wine, the common drink of his time, could represent his blood, soon to be shed. It was also a symbol of the Passover. It represented the blood put on the door posts of the Hebrew houses, so the Lord would "pass over" their houses when the plagues came.

Leader: *We will now share a roll to remember these events. We normally drink tea and coffee at our Pot Luck Suppers. If you wish you may dip your piece of bread in whatever you are drinking. Remember that Jesus told his disciples to use the familiar items on their table to remember him. In the same way we can use our familiar things as we remember.*

(Bread or roll is passed, beginning with the leader(s) and dipped if desired.)

Leader: *I am sure what we have done here tonight has reminded you of the Eucharist, or Holy Communion, which we celebrate as a full church community. Sometimes by transferring concepts to a different setting the action becomes more meaningful. We hope this has happened for you tonight.*

2nd helper: There is something else on this table that has symbolism for me.

Leader: *And what is that?*

2nd helper: I see leftovers. Now don't laugh, because leftovers are something that we should be asking forgiveness for. We have so much, and so many have so little. Shouldn't we say a prayer of confession, as well as a prayer of thanksgiving before we leave?

Leader: *That's an excellent idea. Let us pray:*

CLOSING PRAYER

For all the symbolism of the things on this table, we give you thanks, O God. The salt, the yeast, the mustard seed, the water and the bread all have special meanings for us. We thank you for the power of these symbols and for the way they help us keep the commitment we made when we decided to follow the teaching of your Son, Jesus.

Forgive us, we pray, when we are self-centered; consuming delicious food without remembering those who would be happy to have the leftovers from our tables. Make us good stewards of all that you have given us; help us to share in meaningful ways; and hasten the coming of your Kingdom, when all shall live in peace and children shall not cry in hunger. These things we ask in Jesus' name. Amen.

LENT

20

Tennebrae Service

PREPARATION

This service is most effective when performed in the worship space but it can also be done more informally in a meeting room. Besides the service leader, several helpers are needed, including four readers and others to turn off the overhead lights, as well as musicians (a soloist for a small service or full choir and organ, etc. for a full Good Friday service). As well, four candles and a candle snuffer are central to the service.

WORSHIP

Tennebrae is a German word meaning "from light to darkness." Unlike the Advent wreath, which grows brighter as each candle is lit, in a Tennebrae service candles are extinguished until the sanctuary is in darkness, indicating that we are waiting and preparing ourselves to experience not the joyful birth of the Christ child, but his suffering, his crucifixion, and his death.

In our Lenten time, we look at our own lives, and sometimes we squirm a bit. If we have in some way made a public profession of our faith we recognize that we have not always lived up to the vows we made at that time. During Lent we seek forgiveness and we sometimes deny ourselves, or challenge ourselves, in order to be better prepared for the Good Friday and Easter services.

Some Tennebrae services use seven candles as symbols of the seven deadly sins. Others use four candles, following the path of Jesus to the Cross. Our four candles, however, will be used to symbolize the four aspects of our lives that combine to make us who we are. There are several ways to express these four parts of our lives: the 4H club logo identifies Head, Heart, Hand and Home. The purpose of United Church Women in the United Church is also fourfold, and speaks of Christian Witness, Study, Fellowship and Service. But we will use the designations employed by most psychologists indicating the four parts of our lives as physical, intellectual, emotional and spiritual.

Since only we can confess to God our abuse, misuse, or anxiety about any of these parts of our lives, there will be no words of confession used in our time together. Instead, we will bring into our own consciousness, during one or two minutes of silence, either thanksgiving for that part of our life, confession surrounding it, or a prayer for the enrichment of it. Following the period of silence, the leader will extinguish one candle and say the words **"the light grows dim."** We will respond with the words **"the darkness deepens."**

Hymn
   "Beneath the cross of Jesus"

1st Reader: Matthew 4: 1-11 (Jesus going into the wilderness) **(Pause)**

"I appeal to you therefore, brothers and sisters, by the mercies of God, to present your *bodies* as a living sacrifice, holy and acceptable to God..." (Romans 12:1)

Allow a significant period of silence, then extinguish the first candle.

Leader: The light grows dim.

People: The darkness deepens. **(1st set of lights turned off, if possible)**

2nd Reader: Matthew 22:34-40 (A lawyer tests Jesus) **(Pause)**

"Do not be conformed to this world, but be transformed by the renewing of your *minds*, so that you may discern what is the will of God..." (Romans 12:2)

Another period of silence. The second candle is extinguished.

Leader: The light grows dim.

People: The darkness deepens. **(Next set of lights turned off.)**

Special Music — if desired

3rd Reader: John 11:28-37 (Jesus weeps) **(Pause)**

"I give you a new commandment, that you *love one another*. Just as I have loved you, you also should love one another." (John 13:34)

Silence. The third candle is extinguished.

Leader: The light grows dim.

People: The darkness deepens. **(More lights turned off.)**

4th Reader: Mark 14: 32-41a (Gethsemane) **(Pause)**

"Come to me, all you that are weary and are carrying heavy burdens, and I will give you rest..." (Matthew 11:28)

Silence. The fourth candle is extinguished.

Leader: The light grows dim.

People: The darkness deepens. **(Complete darkness at this point, until a soloist or choir sings:)**

Hymn
  "Were you there"

Lights come up gradually, but only enough for people to see as they leave.

21

All You Who Are Weary

> ### PREPARATION
>
> Depending on the prayer exercise you use during this program, you may need a tape of quiet music, some talented singers in your midst, or a candle.
>
> If a take-home object is desired, there are prayers available on bookmarks, or tiny crosses might be provided, along with the poem "A cross in my pocket" printed in the resource section.

WORSHIP

Call to Worship

"Come to me, all you that are weary and are carrying heavy burdens, and I will give you rest. Take my yoke upon you, and learn from me; for I am gentle and humble in heart, and you will find rest for your souls. For my yoke is easy, and my burden is light." (Matthew 11:28-30) Let us find rest for our souls as we worship together.

Prayer

Sometimes our weariness is not simply tiredness of body, God. Sometimes we feel a heavy weariness in our very souls. Your Son, Jesus, understood this feeling and offered to teach us how to ease the burdens that living in this world places upon us. Let your holy spirit rest gently with us now so that, refreshed in body and soul, we may be energized to be your people in our church and world. Amen.

Hymn

"I heard the voice of Jesus say"

Scripture

John 4:1-6 (or, if desired, continue to verse 42, the story of the woman of Samaria)

REFLECTION

The story of the woman at the well is so familiar that it is easy to pass over the information given in the first verses of the chapter, especially verse six which indicates that Jesus was tired when he met this woman of Samaria. We also tend to forget the fact that Jesus didn't plan to go through Samaria. It was a place that Jews avoided as much as possible and we can imagine how Jesus must have felt about this unpleasant detour in what was a long and tiresome journey. The King James Version of the Bible reads, "Jesus therefore, being wearied with his journey, sat thus on the well."

Picture, then, this weary man, looking for a place to rest and a drink of water, finding himself caught up in a theological discussion with a woman who would be considered untouchable by the men travelling with him. It is also interesting to note that because of this conversation at the well, Jesus was asked to stay in Samaria and he was there for two days (verse forty). These two days would have provided the physical rest that his body craved, as well as the opportunity to preach and teach to a community that might never have heard his message if he hadn't been so tired that he sat down on Jacob's well.

For Jesus, a time of weariness opened up an opportunity to show his disciples once again that there was no one excluded from his love. It was an opportunity to openly admit, for the first time, that he believed he was the long-awaited Messiah. It helped to clarify his thinking, and the result was that he gained an even larger following, and he was able to get some rest before he returned to Galilee. We need to look for golden opportunities that may show up when we least expect them, even when we're tired, weary and discouraged.

Sometimes it seems that the whole church is weary these days. We're tired of committees, we've lost some of the enthusiasm we used to have for new programs. While bible study is the cornerstone of their faith for some people, for others it is a dreary obligation. We grumble about the music in church, everything that's sung is either too old, too new, too fast, or too slow. Many church groups exist only to plan how to raise money. There is a great yearning for something more, something different, some new energy.

There are at least two ways to deal with physical weariness. Actually, they're exactly opposite one another — you can rest, or you can get moving! If, in our church groups, we are thinking about the type of weariness that rest doesn't help, I would say that the recipe is to get moving, to look for opportunities to do something different. Have a brainstorming session and dream up great impossible schemes and then start making at least one of them possible. Start an exercise group, maybe, so that lots of people can get moving. Meet for a walk instead of a meeting. Learn a new hymn and offer to be the choir one Sunday. There are dozens of things you can do if you can shake off weariness.

Weariness of the soul doesn't always respond to rest *or* to exercise. But it may respond to prayer. We have learned recently that doctors are now admitting that prayer is an important supplement to medication or surgery. Prayer can restore our energies and it can calm stress. We need to work at how we pray, because too often we're weary of that too! Maybe we need to find a new book on prayer to read, or to learn the technique of complete relaxation. Meditation, journaling and contemplative silence are forms of prayer that we could explore. All will help ease the weariness of our souls.

Prayer

Help us to be open to the moving of your Spirit, O God; able to hear your voice in the silence, to see your purpose intertwined with the reality of our lives. When we are weary, remind us that your Son offered to share our burdens; when we find it hard to pray, hear the prayers we have locked within our hearts. In Jesus name, Amen.

PROGRAM

The purpose of this program is to practice some prayer techniques that may help to ease the "soul weariness" that modern Christians can experience. Assuming that you have chosen this program because you sense weariness within your group, begin by making sure that everyone is comfortable, knows who is sitting beside them, and that the purpose of the program has been clearly explained.

In a small group, a candle or other worship centerpiece could be provided.

Begin by leading the group in a relaxing exercise. Ask that people close their eyes and make themselves aware of their bodies, beginning with their head and shoulders, arms, back, buttocks, thighs, calves and feet. Ask them to tense each part of their body as you name it, then relax it. Do this two or three times, with some very quiet music in the background, if desired.

When you feel most people are relaxed, ask them to think of a familiar verse from the Bible, possibly some words of Jesus, such as "Come unto me..." "Do not be afraid...." or "Lo, I am with you always... " Then suggest that everyone repeat the phrase in their minds, over and over again. Allow about five minutes for this, and when you feel the time is right bring people back to reality gently, by repeating the body relaxation part, closing with the opening of the eyes.

An alternative suggestion would be to have the group sing the refrain of the hymn "Veni Sancte Spiritus." The refrain should be sung slowly, over and over again, until you as leader indicate the time to return to the group. Again, five minutes would be appropriate, although it may seem like a long time.

When all are comfortable again and aware of one another, ask if anyone would like to share how they felt about this experience. Is it something that they do during their own prayer time, or is it new to them? Did they feel energized by it? Do they consider this as prayer?

If you wish, another prayer exercise could follow. Explain what will happen before you start, indicating that everyone will be asked to focus their attention on a candle while they think of people and situations that they would like to bring before God in prayer. Four or five minutes of silence will follow and *then* people will be asked to name the person or situation they have been thinking about, using the words, "I lift to the light of God ......(name or situation)" Make sure that people understand that only the name or situation is to be spoken, without explanation or details, and that they should allow about thirty seconds of silence between each intercession. When all understand the exercise, proceed as you have indicated. Close with a brief prayer to gather the intercessions together, such as:

Hear the prayers of your people, O God, the words we have spoken, the thoughts that have been in our minds. We lift all of these to the light of your love, through the power of the holy spirit, and through the name of Jesus Christ, the light of the world. Amen.

CLOSING

How you close this program will depend on the intensity — or lack of it — that has been generated by the prayer exercises. Group members may want to talk further, or they may be content to leave or get on with other things. If there are tears they do not need to be explained, and hugs are an appropriate "Amen" to prayer. Even laughter may follow if people have been experiencing something new or different. That's okay too.

General Programs

22

A Golden Program

PREPARATION

This program may be used at any time, but would be particularly appropriate if there is a Golden Anniversary of any sort within your membership. Or, it could be used (with some adaptation) to recognize and celebrate the senior members of your group or community. Chocolate "gold coins" would be an interesting take-home item. Use your imagination if you would like to make this a very special event: yellow name tags, yellow flowers and candles for a worship center and anything else that comes to mind. Enjoy!

Worship

Call to Worship

Gold. From the golden sun that rose on the day we were born, to the golden years that supposedly describe our old age, we are fascinated by this precious metal. It has captured the minds of people ever since the first nugget of yellow ore was separated from its neighboring rock and hammered into coin or jewelry. Lovers have been won by it, gods have been worshipped with it, and wars have been fought over it. How thankful we are that the God whom we worship requires only that we should be just, loving and humble. Let us worship:

Prayer

O God, you are just, you are loving and your Son was the most humble person we have ever known. We have trouble with these requirements, God. We claim we seek justice for all, but only if it doesn't interfere with our own standard of living. We easily love family and friends but find it difficult to love our enemies or the unlovable. And as for humility, we seem to favour things that improve our self image instead. Have mercy upon us, O God, refine us as gold is made pure in the furnace. Shape us into the people we would wish to be, and brighten our lives as the golden sun brightens our world. Amen.

Hymn

"Jesus bids us shine"

Scripture

Matthew 10:5-14

Reflection

When a marriage, organization or a business has existed for fifty years, we celebrate what we call a Golden Anniversary. Because gold has always been treasured, these anniversaries are also very special occasions.

The Bible is also treasured by Christians of every age. There are many references to gold within the pages of the Bible — gold that indicates wealth, gold used in temple furnishings, gold as a source of power. It is interesting to note, however, that only once does Jesus mention gold, and when he did it was in a negative sense. When he sent the disciples out into the country to preach his gospel, he told them *not* to take any gold with them. It seems strange that in a book filled with references to silver and gold, to streets of gold and golden images, the main character sees no need of the precious metal.

It is very easy, therefore, to condemn the pursuit of riches, or power. To say that, like those disciples sent out to do God's will, we should not burden ourselves with money or extra clothes or the latest computer technology. There's a hymn by Jim Manley called "The gifts that you gave me" that says, "O my Lord, free my fingers from possessions that possess me..." and there is much for modern people to consider when it comes to practising their faith while accumulating more and more of this world's goods, whether it be gold or art or real estate.

On the other hand, in these days of stress and technology, there is something golden that we can celebrate whenever we come together as a group of people with a common interest. There is a sense in which *relationships* are the gold of our time, and often these relationships must be made and nurtured within such groups. Few of us have a large circle of close friends in our lives these days. Many do not have extended families living within driving distance, so we no longer go home or have children come every Sunday for lunch, nor do we gather all the aunts and uncles and cousins together for a simple birthday. We're scattered, and the telephone is a wonderful invention, but it can't come close to a hug! It is our service organizations, and our faith communities, that must fill some of the gaps in our close personal relationships. In these groups we work together, we laugh together, we play together. Members of these organizations support us in times of sorrow, illness or despair. Not only are we there for one another, but through our community involvement we often support those in need who do not belong to our organization.

Old autograph books sometimes have an entry that reads, "Make new friends but keep the old, the first are silver, the latter gold." The bonds that hold us together are called golden cords. In the letter of James, in the New Testament, we are warned that gold is not impervious to corruption (James 5:3) and we know that relationships need constant attention in order to retain their glow. As we celebrate **(specific occasion could be mentioned here)** we also accept the challenge to be vigilant and loving so that our important relationships receive the attention they deserve.

Prayer

Gracious and eternal God, we know that you share our joy whenever we celebrate the things that are good and meaningful in our lives. Today we thank you for relationships, for the people who are part of our history, for friends we will make in the future. (Especially ....) We pray that all of our relationships may work together to form an important part of the fabric of your kingdom. Go forward with us, O God, so that future years will be golden ones, years dedicated to fulfilling our own potential as well as making your purpose and will our own. Years of hope and strength. In the name of your Son we pray. Amen.

PROGRAM

Begin with some word association: ask people to suggest phrases that come to mind when they think of the word gold or golden. (golden calf, silver and gold, heart of gold, etc.)

If gold were to represent the most precious thing in our lives, what would be golden for members of the group? (health, family, etc.)

Ask people to share one golden memory — something that happened to them that they will always cherish.

(If this program is used in a party atmosphere, it could end here.)

Bible Study

Re-read the scripture used in the worship period. (Matthew 10:5-14) Have two other people read the same story in the other synoptic gospels (Mark 6:7-13 and Luke 9:1-6). Explain what is meant by synoptic and show how most Bibles give you this information. Note that the word *gold* is an insignificant word in the story, but yet it is the only time that Jesus uses the word.

What would we need to do if we were to take these words as an example to follow? (Preach, heal, travel without money, etc.) Is this realistic for Christians today? If not, is this just an interesting piece of history, or is there still a message for us today? If there is, what is the message?

Which is the most comfortable position to take when reading this story: (1) it happened a long time ago and doesn't apply to us today, or (2) there is a need today for people who are willing to be worker priests, that is, to devote their lives to the challenge Christ presents in this story. People, for example, who would be willing to live on a secular income while engaged in ministry. There is also a third option: (3) recognize that there are worker priests in our society and that if we cannot be like them we can support them. Share an example from your own experience, or use Tom and Anne Gunn's story:

Tom and Anne Gunn both grew up in Cape Breton, a histori-cally and culturally distinct area of Nova Scotia. They were involved in church activities, and both were inspired as teenagers by meeting and hearing Jean Vanier tell the story of L'Arche communities around the world. L'Arche International is made up of many individual communities where mentally and physically challenged people, people rejected by society, live together in a caring, accepting, home.

Following some experience with L'Arche communities in India, Tom and Anne, with the help of a local Board, formed a similar community in Orangedale, Cape Breton in 1982. In some ways it was not like other L'Arche communities, which were normally placed in more urban areas, but it eventually earned the respect of L'Arche International and is now made up of three separate homes that support sixteen core members (mentally or physically challenged persons) and sixteen assistants. Over the years there have been more than sixty people who have been assistants at L'Arche, many of them continue in similar occupations and all have been deeply influenced by the experience.

The Gunn's have eight children, three of whom are adopted, and one who died shortly after birth. Their fourth child, David, who has Down's Syndrome, spent a year in hospital as a baby. The oldest is now seventeen and a new baby arrived in 1995. Anne claims that she is fully liberated since, "I can choose exactly as I want, and I want to be a mother in the home." Their financial situation involves sharing all that they have, completely confident that God will provide for them.

At the sacrament to celebrate their marriage, Tom and Anne used these words to seal their covenant, and they have lived by them ever since:

"We feel called, as our first act of marriage, to enter into a covenant with God, and before you, we do this, trusting not in our own strength, but confident that if we follow God's will, and remain close to rejected persons, He will care for us.

"We feel called to create a Christian family, discovering together what Jesus wants of us — a family of simplicity and welcome, especially for those wounded in their minds and body. We ask you to help us to be true to this and to pray with us that we may always remain faithful to this call."

Following the stories, it may be necessary to assure group members that such lifestyles are rare and beautiful but we should not let them discourage us from living out our own lives in what we may consider much more mundane ways. We can love and support people who have chosen to dedicate their whole lives to serving others, but we should not feel guilty because we have followed a different path.

CLOSING

In a L'Arche community people must depend on one another, just as Jesus' disciples depended on the generosity of the communities they visited. What or who do we depend on in our everyday lives? Ask people to make suggestions: the oil company, banks, grocery stores, etc.

23

Moving Experiences

PREPARATION

If you are using this program at a time when someone is moving away, or someone has recently joined your group, it might be interesting to have some simple souvenir of your church or community for the guests of honour.

If there are no current moves, you might provide seeds of an easy-care house plant, and suggest that people remember the importance of their "roots" each time they water it.

WORSHIP

Call to Worship

God does not often call people to go back, except to repent of our sins. Following repentance, God's call is always urging us forward, moving us in new directions. Sometimes the people of

God answer with a brave "yes, Lord, we're on our way." Occasionally we move reluctantly and quite possibly there are times when we don't even hear the message. Let us respond to God's call at this time, by offering our worship and praise.

Prayer
God of all our journeys, help us to hear your voice. Be with us when our travels lead us into valleys or deserts, rejoice with us when we arrive safely at our destination and are warmly greeted by those we love. Keep us moving, keep us growing, give us wings. Keep us centered, keep us faithful, give us roots. Amen.

Hymn
"To Abraham and Sarah"

Scripture
Genesis 31:13-21

REFLECTION

When Jacob and Rachel fled from Rachel's father, they took the usual paraphernalia of moving with them — farm equipment and animals, clothing, furniture. It was Rachel, however, who was determined to take something of great value to her — the household gods that represented her heritage. In actual fact she had to steal these items, and the way she hid them to keep her father from finding them is a very interesting story in itself. We will return to that later in our program.

When modern families move they usually discover that there are certain things they *must* take with them. Often useless, sometimes cumbersome, these items, like Rachel's household gods, represent our family history, and they are very important to us.

A popular slogan of the nineties urges parents to give their children "roots and wings." We all need things in our lives that do not change: a family heirloom. a particular picture or piece of

GENERAL

furniture. Also we also need to know the constancy of our parents' love, and God's love. Most of us have a certain place we can call home, so that no matter how often we move there is always one spot that has a special meaning or value for us.

Wings, however, give us the ability to leave that special place, to venture into new locations, to learn new things, to meet new people, possibly to go "where no one has gone before." As another slogan says, "Sure you can fly, but that cocoon has to go!" Roots are much more comfortable than wings. There is security in being rooted, there is insecurity and fear involved in the risky business of flying.

There is a man, ninety years old, who is still living in the house in which he was born. His wife has shared sixty-six of those years with him. In contrast, their oldest son has moved 20 times during the first 39 years of his marriage. What a difference in lifestyles! The older couple have friends and memories that revolve around their community, their school, their church. They love to greet people who have moved away but come back to visit. They tell stories of people long dead, but whose memory is kept alive because there are still those who knew them. Their son has made friends too, but they are scattered all around the country. Since his wife has roots in a different area his children regard their grandparents' farm with more nostalgia than they have for any of the various places they lived. They, like so many of today's children, were transients, constantly having to go to new schools, find new friends, leaving behind much that they treasured.

Finding a new faith community when you move may involve going to the local church of your denomination, if there is only one, or doing some shopping around if there are several. If you have to choose, it is quite likely that you will choose the congregation that makes you feel most welcome, the one you sense will provide a place for you to belong. It is comforting to know that wherever you worship you will be worshipping the same familiar God, the One who was present in the place you left, and is not only with you, but has gone before you. You will catch a glimpse of God when a neighbour calls, when you consider joining the choir, or when you're asked to help at the church supper. Whether you live a life of permanence, or a life of transience, making the stranger welcome can be a personal enrichment.

Prayer

Root us in your love, O God, so that we have the confidence to reach out in new directions. Give us courage to learn new things, to meet new people, to expose ourselves to new ideas. Whether we move physically, intellectually, emotionally or spiritually, help us to understand that the ability to change, to think, to feel and to commune with you are all gifts of your spirit. May we use them to grow ever closer to you, through your Son Jesus, and through the continual presence of the Holy Spirit. Amen.

PROGRAM

Begin by sharing stories around the moving theme: experiences with moving trucks, feelings of loneliness in a new community, or ways in which your group attempts to greet newcomers.

Do some brainstorming around stories of people moving in the Bible. You will come up with many. In addition to Jacob and Rachel, people will remember from the Old Testament the travels of Adam and Eve leaving the Garden, Abraham and Sarah venturing forward to the Promised Land, Moses leading the slaves out of Egypt, Joseph's journey into slavery, Naaman's trip to seek healing from the prophet Elisha, and more. In the New Testament there is the trip to Bethlehem by Mary and Joseph, the journey of the Magi, all of Jesus' travels to teach, heal and preach, and Paul's missionary travels. The Bible often seems like a huge travelogue!

GENERAL

Provide Bibles or photocopies of the story of Rachel stealing the household gods in Chapter 31 of Genesis, verses 1-42. Use the following questions to bring out the significant points in the story:

1. Why did Jacob decide to move?
2. Why did Leah and Rachel agree with this move?
3. Why did Rachel want to take the household gods (Teraphim) with her?
4. Where did she hide them?
5. Did Jacob know she had them?
6. What did Jacob say would happen if they were found in his tent?
7. Why didn't her father discover them?

Ask if this story is familiar to your members. If it isn't, can they surmise why? How do we feel about Rachel's theft — was it wrong for her to want to take some of her family history with her? Do you think her bitterness about her father's attitude had anything to do with her decision?

Closing

Conclude your program by standing in a circle, holding hands if that is comfortable for your group, and have each member share one thing which they would refuse to leave behind if they had to move tomorrow.

Remember that Good-bye is a shortened form of "God be with you," a suitable benediction if one is required.

24

Yard Sales

PREPARATION

This program could be used to stir up interest in a yard sale, as part of a series on environmental issues, or just for fun. If there is no yard sale being planned, you could create interest in the program by suggesting that each person bring one item, in good condition, that they no longer need or want. Place them all on a table and instead of selling them, give each person a number and let people take one item from the table as their number is called. You will need to have slips of paper prepared with numbers from one to the number expected.

Provide a flip chart and markers for the discussion section of the program.

WORSHIP

Call to Worship

We believe that God is everywhere, even at yard sales. Let us therefore acknowledge God's presence with us right now, as we worship together.

Prayer

Creator God, your presence with us in times of fun and relaxation is important to us. We want you to be part of everything we do; we want to see something of your will and purpose for your creation in our efforts to recycle as well as in our efforts to communicate with you. We thank you for all the things we use and enjoy and we pray that we may be good caretakers of all that you have provided. In Jesus name we pray, Amen.

Hymn

"All things bright and beautiful"

Scripture

Matthew 7:1-11

REFLECTION

Chapters five, six and seven of the Gospel of Matthew are a collection of Jesus' teachings. Called the Sermon on the Mount, or simply the Teachings of Jesus; these may or may not have been things that were actually said by Jesus in a continuous sermon or in one particular place. They are, however, teachings that are central to the Christian faith, and they contain some of the most well-known and beloved verses in the Bible.

Verse six of the seventh chapter says, "Do not give what is holy to dogs; and do not throw your pearls before swine, or they will trample them underfoot and turn and maul you." Saying something twice, using different words, is a common literary tool in the Bible. Giving what is holy to dogs and throwing pearls before swine, are two examples the same thing. Pearls were considered by ancient people to be the most precious of gems. If we believe that everything God created is holy we can see that this portion of Scripture teaches us that *nothing* should be wasted. We must quickly add that if this is what we believe, the dogs and pigs are holy also, but the food given to animals, which is again holy, is the food that is best suited to their needs, not something that should be used for some other purpose. In verse nine we read that if a child asks for bread, no parent will give that child a stone. There are appropriate and inappropriate ways to respond to need.

These thoughts can help us understand the popularity of yard sales. Don't throw good household items to the dogs or into the landfill: someone may be able to use them. The pearl you have ceased to value may be like a precious stone to someone who needs it.

Yard sale fanatics are sure that God must smile on sunny Saturday mornings when so many cheerful people gather in neighbourhoods all across the country. They are searching for something they need, or hoping to find someone's discarded trash, which can become their precious treasure.

Prayer

We know, dear God, that there are much more serious subjects for us to study, more important issues for our prayers. Laughing God, accept our fun and games as you cherish our faithful devotion to prayer and worship. We thank you for peaceful neighbourhoods everywhere and we pray that the sense of community generated in our yard sales will give us renewed appreciation of our communion with you. Amen.

PROGRAM

In a light-hearted way make a list (on flip chart if possible) of familiar Bible verses that could be used to support the concept of yard sales. Here are some suggestions, if none is forthcoming from the group:

- Cleansing of the Temple (Jesus didn't like merchants making excessive profits)
- Turning water into wine (one person's junk is another person's treasure)
- Rubbing clay on the blind man's eyes (using ordinary things for extraordinary purposes)
- The clay and the potter (making good use of something that seems useless)
- Paul and friends escaping jail in a basket (alternative uses for familiar objects)

Ask people who have never been to a yard sale and have no interest in such things to sit on one side of the room. Ask those who think such adventures illustrate community, thrift and fun, to sit on the other. If there are those who want to hear both sides have them sit in the center.

Have an impromptu debate: invite opinions from each side alternately, pro and con on the subject of yard sales. If you have undecided people, ask them if the debate has convinced them, one way or the other.

To conclude your discussion, get a little more serious and discuss poverty and yard sales. For instance, if someone cannot afford to buy a new toaster, would they feel better about picking up one at a yard sale for two dollars or asking their social worker where one might be available? Are there people in your group who prefer to donate their goods to charity — for second-hand stores or rummage sales — rather than have their own sale? Why? How do members feel about people buying things cheaply at a yard sale and then selling them at a higher price at a local flea market? Does it make a difference if this is done by someone trying to make a little extra money or by a professional dealer in second-hand goods? And what does the increased interest in yard sales have to say about our country's economy?

CLOSING

If you have asked people to bring yard sale type articles to the meeting, begin at the first number and have people go to the table where these have been place and choose one item. Followed by number two, three, etc.

OR — Invite everyone to participate in a yard sale — set time and place. (This could be a group activity or just one person's private sale.)

Extra Resources

Opening Prayers

Opening a meeting with prayer is easy for some people, very difficult for others. For those who need some help with this task, this chapter contains some opening prayers.

These prayers are sometimes called Invocation Prayers, and the basic outline is very easy to follow. Remember the outline and you will soon be composing prayers for any occasion.

1. Address the prayer to God, using a word or phrase of adoration.
2. Include something about the nature of God.
3. Be specific about what you want God to do.
4. Tell God why you want this, and what you hope it will accomplish.
5. Acknowledge that you pray in the name of Jesus, or through the Trinity.
6. Encourage everyone to say "Amen," which means "So be it," to indicate that all join you in the prayer.

For example:

Gracious God,

you were with Noah when he built the Ark, and you have been with many people throughout history as they built places of worship.

141

RESOURCES

Be with us today as we make plans to enlarge our church hall.

We pray that our children will come to know and love you as they meet together each week in bright and cheerful rooms.

We ask your guidance in the name of Jesus, who loves all children.
Amen.

MORE PRAYERS TO OPEN A MEETING

Almighty God, source of all truth, all wisdom, make us aware of your presence among us. Help us feel that what we are doing here today is an important part of your will and purpose for your people. Remind us that whether the task is large or small, it is worthy of doing well. We ask this in Jesus name. Amen.

Gracious God, your name is Love and in love we gather this day to participate in the work of our church. Keep us focused, we pray, as ideas are shared and plans are made. Help us work together, to put personal preferences aside for the sake of the whole community, to truly feel that we are one in the bonds of love. Amen.

Loving God, thank you for the sense of humour that you placed in the hearts and minds of your people. Help us to see the funny side in our deliberations this day, keep us from taking ourselves and our work too seriously. We want to do this work, dear God, we know that it needs to be done, but it will be planned much quicker and equally as well if we approach it with a joyous attitude. We ask this in the name of Jesus whose humanity must surely have included laughter. Amen.

Creator God, source of all that is good and lovely, we give you thanks for the beauty that surrounds us, in the forests, seas and mountains **(or lakes and hills)** as well as in the lives of those we love. Fill us with wonder, O God, and may our prayers of thanksgiving inspire us to share your love with others, to spread the good news that the One who has created us will never forsake us. In Jesus name, Amen.

Compassionate God, who looks with love on the sorrows of your people, our hearts are heavy because there is sadness in our midst. We seek the comfort of your presence, we ask for understanding and compassion. Help us to be your tears as we cry together, help us to be your arms as we hold one another. We ask this in the name of Jesus, who knew so well the face of human suffering. Amen.

God of the eagle and God of the humming bird, God of the moose and the mouse, the variety within your creation is awe inspiring. Help us to see the variety of gifts available to your church within this place, help us to acknowledge each of them with love and thanks. As we affirm each other and the contributions we make, we pray that we will be inspired to offer all that we have and are to honour and glorify your name. Through Christ our Lord. Amen.

A Lay Person's Dictionary of Prayer

Invocation, or Call to Worship: Acknowledging God's presence at this particular time. It is not necessary to ask God to be present, since God is always with us.

Prayer of Approach: A prayer that acknowledges God's presence, and draws our attention to the liturgy that follows.

Prayer of Confession: This prayer directs our thoughts to how we have failed to achieve our full potential as children of God. We admit that we have sinned and ask God to forgive us.

Assurance of Pardon: The presider assures the people that God *does* forgive our sins. This is often followed by a Doxology, or other prayer response to indicate the joy we experience as forgiven people, and to praise God for that forgiveness.

Adoration: A time to lift hearts and voices in praise and adoration to our God. Sometimes this is simply an adjective placed before God's name at the beginning of the prayer, such as "Almighty God," or a phrase immediately following God's name — "God, we praise you for your loving kindness towards us..."

Thanksgiving: An opportunity to express our thanks to God for God's generosity towards us.

Supplication: A specific prayer for God's help, comfort, or strength.

Intercession: Prayer for others.

Commissioning: Words of challenge, used to send the worshippers from the sanctuary into the world.

Benediction: The good words or blessing that the presider uses to close a service of worship. There are many different benedictions, but most use the triune formula in some way, referring to God as "Father, Son and Holy Spirit." Many people who favour inclusive language now use terms such as "Creator, Redeemer, Sustainer" for God.

Resources

The book *Approaches to Prayer* edited by Henry Morgan and published by Moorhouse Publishing, Box 1321, Harrisburg, PA 17105, is an excellent resource book for anyone wishing to practice prayer and considering new ways of praying.

For those interested in looking at prayer in a more in-depth fashion, *Two Ways of Praying*, by Paul F. Bradshaw is available in Canada from the United Church Publishing House and in the United States from Abingdon Press.

Talent Money

There's always something coming up that costs a lot of money,
How we wish to could make our own, just like the bees make honey!
That will not work, we need to give, and use our talents too,
That's why these two little dollars are coming now to you.

Take the money, and think quite hard, about your talents true,
Then use your talent, use your head, think of something you can do
To make this money grow a bit, double it or more,
We don't however recommend you take it and just store.

In one month's time we'll meet again, the usual time and place,
And we'll see how much our funds have grown, although it's not a race!
Tell us how you used your talents, share with us your skills,
Did you build, or decorate, or make a batch of dills?

Whatever you do, you can be sure, we'll thank you, yes indeed,
You'll help us raise some money, that we do surely need.
And you'll use your talents, given by God, in some creative ways,
We'll all give thanks for all our gifts, and praise God all our days.

Name: _____

Phone Number: _____

I made my $2.00 grow to $_____ and here is how I did it:

_____

_____

_____

_____

_____

_____

**(Add something here to give the name of a contact person,
and some indication of why the money is being raised.)**

The Cross in my Pocket

I carry a cross in my pocket, a simple reminder to me
Of the fact that I am a Christian, no matter where I may be.
This little cross is not magic, nor is it a good luck charm,
It isn't meant to protect me from every physical harm.
It's not for identification for all the world to see,
It's simply an understanding between my Saviour and me.
When I put my hand in my pocket to bring out a coin or a key
The cross is there to remind me of the price Christ paid for me.
It reminds me, too, to be thankful for my blessings day by day,
And to strive to serve God better in all that I do and say.
It's also a daily reminder of the peace and comfort I share
With all who know my Master and give themselves to His care.
So, I carry a cross in my pocket reminding no one but me
That Jesus Christ is Lord of my life if only I'll let Him be.

This poem, or variations of it, has been around for a long time. Apologies to anyone who might recognize it as something they have written. It is usually photocopied and given to a friend, or members of a group, along with a small cross. Sometimes a small purchased cross is used, or some have used various craft materials to make this symbol of our faith.

If you wish, the poem can be reduced to two lines, which can easily be memorized:

I carry a cross in my pocket, reminding no one but me
That Jesus Christ is all I need, no matter where I may be.

Scripture Index

Hymn Index

Hymn Index

Song	Page	Source
To show by touch and word	28	SGP/VU
Veni Sancte Spiritus	116	SGP/VU
What a friend we have in Jesus	12	HB/VU
Were you there	111	HB/VU

Suggested hymns are taken from the following sources:

ES   *Everflowing Streams, Songs for Worship*, Ruth C. Duck and Michael G. Bush, editors (New York: The Pilgrim Press, 1981), p. 72.

GH   *Great Hymns of the Church* (Hope Publishing Co. 1966).

HB   *The Hymn Book of the Anglican Church of Canada and The United Church of Canada*, authorized by General Synod and General Council, 1971.

SGP *Songs for a Gospel People: A Supplement to The Hymn Book (1971)*, R. Gerald Hobbs, ed. (Winfield, B.C.: Wood Lake Books, 1987).

SOG *Songs of the Gospel*, published for The United Church of Canada by Gordon V. Thompson Ltd., Toronto, 1948, #134.

VU   *Voices United: The Hymn and Worship Book of the United Church of Canada*, John Ambrose, ed. (Etobicoke, Ontario: The United Church Publishing House, 1996).

Also of interest from
The United Church Publishing House

Program Ready:
23 Quick and Complete Programs for the Church Year
Dorothy MacNeill
A collection of programs for every season throughout the church year with ready material for worship, reflection, and discussion. Each program is presented as a complete service and includes a call to worship, scripture, prayers, hymn suggestions, and a short reflection, as well as ideas to spark group activities and discussion.

Joy Is Our Banquet: Resources for Everyday Worship
Keri K. Wehlander
The refreshing, sometimes startling, images contained in this resource highlight themes such as patience, friendship, beginnings, and money, affirming the everyday experiences that are an integral part of what is holy in life. Each of the liturgies is complete, with prayers, litanies, hymn suggestions, and biblical passages. This volume is poetic and accessible, nurturing and giving expression to the spiritual journey of all who use it.

There is a Season:
Meditations for Private and Group Worship
Betty Radford Turcott
The themes of justice, peace, and hope are explored in these inspirational devotions, which follow the church year. Each service is complete on two facing pages and includes a call to worship, opening prayer, scripture, suggested popular hymns, a brief meditation, and closing prayer. Suitable for both personal devotion and group worship.

Also of interest from The United Church Publishing House

Telling Her Story: Theology Out of Women's Struggles
Lois Miriam Wilson
"I want to find a way to reconcile my profound love and debt
to the biblical record with my emerging awareness of women's
struggles towards wholeness. I want to communicate these
learnings to children before they get any older," states Wilson.
Her popular book is an ideal resource for those who wish to
bring new ears and eyes to biblical stories.

Images of Ourselves:
The Faith and Work of Canadian Women
photos by Pamela Harris
A book to celebrate The Ecumenical Decade of Churches in
Solidarity with Women in Church and Society, *Images of Ourselves* is an acknowledgement and appreciation of the lives and
work of women. Included are a gathering of prayers, poems,
songs, meditations, and photographs that provides a powerful
tool for devotion and renewal.

Crucified Woman
Doris Jean Dyke
In this short and moving book, theologian Doris Jean Dyke tells
the powerful story of the impact a statue of a crucified woman
had on members of the church and university communities in
downtown Toronto. For many, initial feelings of outrage
evolved into new feelings and thoughts about traditional
Christian doctrine.